6.00

How
To Trace
Your Family
History

How To Trace Your Family History

Bill R. Linder

Everest House
Publishers   New York

This book is dedicated to GRANDPARENTS—all of them everywhere—particularly to my own grandparents, Mattie Shaw and Will Yeater, Ida Taylor and Christopher (Kit) Linder—and my wife's grandparents, Callie Catherine Pate and Virgil Stephens, Pearl Stoker and Albert James; but this work is a special tribute to my children's grandparents—Maxine and Royce Linder and Frances and Virgil James, who have made life for me and my family a joy and considerably more productive with their examples, encouragement, and love.

Acknowledgments

Special acknowledgment and thanks are due the following friends who generously commented on the manuscript: Dr. Neil D. Thompson, attorney at law, Fellow, American Society of Genealogists (F.A.S.G.), New York City (who contributed heavily to the chapters on evaluation of information and heraldry); Richard S. Lackey, F.A.S.G., businessman and genealogical editor and writer, Forest, Mississippi; Winston De Ville, F.A.S.G., genealogical publisher, New Orleans; my father-in-law, Dr. Virgil A. James, executive development educator and management consultant, Little Rock; my journalist friend Colleen J. Heninger, Vienna, Virginia; and my sweet, patient, and supportive wife Nancy. Thanks are also due to Becky, Martha, Richard, Bobby Jack, and Callie—who gave up many hours of playtime with their father. Bobby Jack asked one night, "Daddy, why do you always make so many books?" After that comment, the manuscript was delayed for an evening!

BILL R. LINDER

Vienna, Virginia

Contents

part three
METHODOLOGY—HOW TO DO IT
EFFICIENTLY AND EFFECTIVELY

part four
HIRING OR BECOMING A SKILLED
GENEALOGIST

part one
Get To Know Your Family And Its "Records"

1
Bring On The Grandparents

"Why don't our grandparents live with us the way they live with their children and grandchildren in the storybooks?"

"Why can't we have them to be with us and to talk to?"

A lack of companionship with grandparents has led to these unexpected complaints against modern society by the current generation of teenagers. Today's teenagers miss traditional grandparents. They want them to be as much of their routine as Saturday night dates.

One researcher says, "They want grandparents like kids had fifty years ago, and they feel something is missing in their neat little suburban houses without them."

"Many teenagers feel very lonely," reports a counseling agency. "They are not sure who they are, why they are on earth, or where they are going. They're searching for identity."

What is it about grandparents that helps to fill voids in our lives—especially the lives of young people? Is it the wisdom of years and experience, that sure-footed confidence and firm approach to reality, or is it the tactful, well-offered advice that often brings a wink of thanks in ticklish situations?

Grandparents play many roles in family affairs. They serve as a link between the child and the preceding generation, bringing continuity to the family and knowledge of previous eras. Through grandparent companionship, the child learns the human qualities and early experiences of his parents. The child has something on which to build his own personality and attitudes—different and separate, yet part of his family unit. The youngster learns to observe the aging process and to accept and enjoy life, regardless of the illness he sees and the eventual death of the aged members of the family.

These older folks who talk about the horse and buggy and kerosene lamps, but who cannot comprehend modern fashions, music, or dance, are merely partial looking-glasses. They reflect the same basic image today's youth will take on years hence. And if you want your fortune told, ask Grandma. She's no soothsayer, but grandparents know what the future will bring if we do this or that or if we don't. They know the secrets of living; they have discovered by the hand-me-down route the all-important clues to finding continuity and purpose in life. The family chain is, by nature, eternal, and each succeeding generation brings a fresh harvest of wisdom and experience, but even our grandparents' grandparents had to learn for themselves the basic lessons in life. Today we live by practically the same codes they did.

Today's teenagers are likely to live until 2030 or 2040. In their middle years they will see a brand new century come, the 21st century, with its revolutionary new ways, means, schemes, and ideas. By then, the present after-school service station attendants and baby-sitters will be struggling to get their own children through college, or may be shifting into an entirely different gear of living as grandparents themselves.

They'll rub elbows, personally, with two centuries, fore and aft. They will have heard their grandparents quote yarns about the Civil War, which they got from their elders, and the Gay

Nineties to them were just that close. Mom and Dad remember well the Great Depression, and the names Goebbels, Himmler, and Hiroshima. The kids will hear first-hand accounts about Korea and Viet Nam and the Bay of Tonkin.

Today's teenagers will eventually know their own grandchildren and will look into their futures, which may extend on into the latter half of the 21st century. Today is literally linked with yesterday and tomorrow.

Parents ought to heed the complaints of today's teenagers and give them back their grandparents. Help them find their "family." Treat them to the fullness of family life only the extended family can offer. A Sunday at grandmother's is a pleasant day to remember, but one day is not enough. Arrange visits—in both your home and theirs—for not only a day or an evening but for several days at a time, and often. It takes a while to get past the superficial hellos and chit-chat and down to real communicating—the kind of relationshiping that only happens when you do things together for a good while. Once into communication, the youngsters will get a chance to evalute the relationships Mom and Dad have with their parents, and by watching these reactions and interrelationships, they can better gauge their own actions.

Invite the grandparents to talk. Nothing pleases them more than to be enthusiastically asked to tell of things that happened "way back when." Buried in those pleasant remembrances, they'll be clueing your kids in on a valuable common sense observation—while Grandpa talks, the children will get a brief glimpse of themselves fifty years from now. This is not a new idea. Carved in stone at the the entrance to our National Archives, boldly proclaimed in the words of Shakespeare, is the profound phrase, "What is past is prologue."

Yes, let's bring on the grandparents, and find out more about them and their people—and ourselves.

15

2
Beginning
Your Search

Your search began when you cast those first wondering thoughts in the grandparent direction. Where did they come from? Why? What were they like when they were young? The answers to these questions are tremendously interesting and worth seeking. They will lead you to stronger family ties, a greater sense of family pride, a keener understanding of self, and a lifegiving fulfillment and satisfaction in really knowing who you are and from whence you came. You will achieve—*identity*.

You will discover definite information about people who helped make you what you are as you stitch yourself to countless generations of ancestors who preceded you. You will become a vehicle for carrying your family history to future generations for their enjoyment and benefit. Your search, of course, will require some basic but simple knowledge of genealogical and family history research methods and sources, the kind of information this book and more advanced ones like it contain.

The extent of involvement and the degree to which people

are productive at genealogy and family history vary with the amount of interest and motivation and the time available. You can do a little or a lot. It's up to you. The information here is designed to help you either way. If you are only mildly curious, this book will acquaint you with genealogy and family history and walk you though the basics of getting some worthwhile projects underway. The stress is on action—actually doing something—getting information down and creating something to show others, even if you produce only a few pages or only one short research paper. On the other hand, if you are seriously interested and want to dig in at research, the information here will give you a good beginning, initiate good habits, and point you in the right direction so that you can work and train eventually to become as skilled as anyone.

In genealogy, we start with ourselves, the known, and work toward the unknown. We first find out all the vital information we can about our parents, and write it down systematically, then we find out about our grandparents, great-grandparents, great-great-grandparents, and on back.

We are concerned with abstracting from the many and varied documents of recorded history four key items: *names, dates, places,* and *relationships.* These are the facts the family searcher uses to build genealogies. People can be identified in records by their names, the dates of events in their lives (birth, marriage, death), the places they lived, and by relationships to others either stated or implied in the records.

The place to begin the search is at home. There you can find information in family bibles, newspaper clippings, birth and death certificates, diaries, letters, scrapbooks, and other memorabilia. You then move outward and visit or write those in your family, particularly older relatives, who may have information. Often, others before you have gathered data about the families in which you are interested. You will thus need to make a survey— by letter, personal visit, or telephone—to find out about such persons and what information is already collected. Before launching your research program further afield into libraries and archives, you will search for distant relatives who may have already done research—perhaps relatives you have never before met. You will learn how to look for them by advertising in the local genealogical bulletins (city, county, and state) where your ancestors lived, or in national genealogical publications.

After exhausting the home, close-relative, and distant-relative sources, you will embark on an adventure of by-mail and in-person research at the many records depositories. You will often be surprised and amazed at what records exist and, at the other extreme, heartbroken to learn of neglect and destruction of records. You will learn about access to existing records, services provided by libraries and archives, and how the available records can help you.

If life up to now or the days of late have been slow or uninteresting, you have caught the right train—for a change! Once aboard the genealogical express, days pace away and hours fade into a collage of nostalgia, talk, reading, meeting new people, writing letters, smiling, studying, working, correcting, driving, compiling and writing, laughing, even crying—as you create a record of people you love or will learn to love and who you want to go on living—if only on paper—for a long, long time.

Home and Family Sources

Simple logic suggests you should start with yourself and work back from the known to the unknown. You automatically know to look through the records at home, at your parents' home, the homes of other close relatives, and the family cemetery. This you should do first. Make your own list of places to look, then start looking.

List of Possible Home Sources

Diaries

Journals

Family bibles

Letters

Scrapbooks

Wedding books

Baby books

Funeral books

School yearbooks

Account books

Business and financial papers

Photograph albums

Backs of photographs

Inside old books (items tucked away, inscriptions, and notes made inside the covers)

Certificates (birth, marriage, death, military, school, church, etc.)

Announcements and invitations (birth, wedding, and graduation)

Newspaper clippings

Autograph books

Artifacts (names on quilts or on backs or bottoms of items)

Now that your thinking process has been kindled, you can see there are many things to look for at home. Use the above list as a guide to help you think of other places to look.

A Few Quick Tips at the Outset

The sooner you begin working the better. Experience, as in nearly all fields, is one of the best teachers in genealogy, too. The following few tips will help you take good first steps.

Squeeze all the information out of your home sources.   It is easy to pass over clues elusively buried in the items around the house. Be alert. As an example, an old letter might mention "Aunt Rosy Murphree." This is valuable information. If the letter says, "Aunt Rosy Murphree went with us over to Sarepta to visit Grandpa Shaw," you have even more information. In only a few words in the old letter, there are present the four key elements of genealogy (names, dates, places, and relationships). Hopefully the letter is dated. You have the names Aunt Rosy Murphree and Grandpa Shaw with stated relationships, that is, the aunt and grandfather of the writer of the letter, and you have the place where Grandpa Shaw lived. See how loaded a letter can be! You have to train yourself to watch for such clues. You also have to learn to check the clues for accuracy, e.g., was "Aunt Rosy" really an aunt, or was she just called aunt?

For another example consider newspaper obituaries—also a fruitful source. Genealogists use care when working with newspapers because the information is provided by people who may have only assumed they knew a person's (family) background. Obituaries, too, normally contain names, dates, places, and relationships. Read carefully for each detail. The closing statement of the obituary may lead you to a cemetery where other family members are buried. Read all the way to the end. In turn, the gravestones in the cemetery may provide further information and possibly more leads. See how the family quest reads like a detective story—one lead leads to another!

Always look for family bibles.   Be alert to the existence of a family bible, especially when you visit older relatives. Remember that such books are often treasures to those who own them, and treat them with respect. Other books may also have family information—an old hymnal or farm account book has more than once recorded an entire family's dates of birth, marriage, and death.

Look in hidden places.   The simple statement, "The mother of Daniel Ashby Shive was the daughter of Henry Ashby," found on the back of an old photograph in South Texas helped solve a difficult genealogical problem. As the migration pattern of the family was uncovered, the marriage of a John Shive and Rebecca Ashby was found in a Kentucky county where a man named Henry Ashby lived. Watch for such clues! Hang onto them when you find them, as you never know when the clue will be used as a lead to a breakthrough in your search.

Really listen when you talk to relatives.   A simple statement of fact or even a guess which might at first seem unimportant can become quite significant as other information is collected. When great-aunt Aggie Mae says, "I believe Grandmother Star-nes was a Williams before she married," take note. And don't forget to write down that it was Aunt Aggie Mae who told you, and note the date of your interview. This will become the very first lead that will embark you on a journey of discovery of your Williams family heritage. For the author, this actual Williams lead eventually produced a claim to descendancy from John Knox, the famous fiery Scottish minister and pioneer of Presbyterianism.

Some information you gather will be wrong.   A good principle to keep in mind is that reliability of information is generally related to the closeness of the informant to the subject. If a man's death certificate gives his birth date as 4 May 1834, but his marriage record shows it to be 4 May 1836, the second is more likely to be correct. Pause and think that through for a minute. It is a basic principle to learn. The record made which is closer to the event is usually the more reliable. However, there are exceptions, and especially at the beginning you should take down all the information you can find, even when the facts are contradictory.

Make complete notes of your sources. Be sure you always make note of the source of every item of fact you find. There is nothing more frustrating than trying later to retrace your steps when you have forgotten where you found something.

Record information as you find it. Over the years genealogists have learned by experience to take down what they find exactly as they find it. Spellings of names of people and places have varied greatly over the years. County boundaries have shifted. Nicknames and abbreviations may stand for something other than what you expect. The handwriting of the person born in Germany or Denmark may be very different and easily misread. Some numbers used to be written differently than they are today. You are never wrong to copy exactly. If in doubt, get a photocopy of the document for your files whenever possible.

Start Out Organized

As you move well into your search, you will want to use the forms genealogists have developed over the years to assist them. These forms will be discussed later (see the separate chapter entitled "The Genealogist's Tools"). However, you can and should start compiling right now. Go ahead and begin without the forms if you don't have copies or ready access to them. Simply list the information you find on sheets of paper. See the illustrated samples.

Start with a page describing your own family. Note the types of information recorded in the "John Hamilton Doe" sample and note the format for recording the information. Dates are recorded in the order of the day, month, and year: 17 Feb. 1940. Names are written in full, using the maiden surnames of females. Places are recorded in the order of town, county, and state.

JOHN HAMILTON DOE

John Hamilton Doe, son of Thomas Hamilton Doe and Margaret Ann Smith, was born 6 May 1930 at Doeville, Cushing Co., Vt. He married 15 June 1955 at Maryville, Randolph Co., Conn., Allison Jane Jones, who was born 2 Feb 1932 at Johnson City, Davenport Co., N.Y., a daughter of Stephen Heninger Jones and Malynna Mae Coffey. Their children were:

1. *John Smith Doe*, b. 14 Mar 1957, Sampson City, Sterling Co., Tex., md. 6 June 1977, San Antonio, Bexar Co., Tex., Shawna Jan Hylton.

2. *Wayne Gene Hamilton Doe*, b. 27 May 1959, Sampson City, Sterling Co., Tex.

3. *Elda Margaret Doe*, b. 13 June 1962, Doeville, Cushing Co., Vt.

4. *June Kathryn Doe*, b. 22 Aug 1965, Doeville, Cushing Co., Vt., d. 17 Nov 1966 at Doeville, bur. Pilgrim's Rest Cemetery, Doeville.

SOURCES: The above information was obtained from the John Hamilton Doe family bible (in his possession); from personal knowledge of Mrs. Margaret Smith Doe; and from the marriage announcement and newspaper account of the marriage of child no. 1, John Smith Doe.*

The ancestry chart shown maps out your ancestry, sketching the roadways into the past. You can draw the ancestry chart with a ruler. The chart looks like a sports tournament plan turned backward. Whereas the whole-family page (John Hamilton Doe example) brings out more information about each ancestral family, the ancestry chart reflects a person's direct ancestry. To get started, draw up a several-generation ancestry chart and then

*This is a simplified statement regarding sources. Usually more detail is desired. The chapter on "Notetaking and Filing" gives instructions on how to construct proper source references.

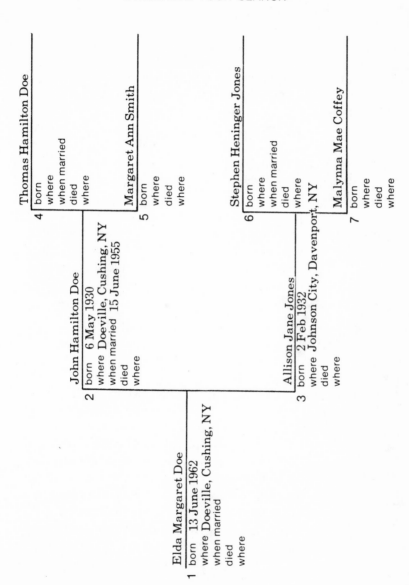

4 Thomas Hamilton Doe
born
where
when married
died
where

5 Margaret Ann Smith
born
where
died
where

2 John Hamilton Doe
born 6 May 1930
where Doeville, Cushing, NY
when married 15 June 1955
died
where

6 Stephen Heninger Jones
born
where
when married
died
where

7 Malynna Mae Coffey
born
where
died
where

3 Allison Jane Jones
born 2 Feb 1932
where Johnson City, Davenport, NY
died
where

1 Elda Margaret Doe
born 13 June 1962
where Doeville, Cushing, NY
when married
died
where

25

make a complete page(s) of information on the whole immediate families of each ancestral couple shown on the chart.

From what you know and what you find around home, you can start right now and put down on paper quite a bit of information that would probably fill at least one ancestry chart and several family group pages. You can, at the very moment you finish reading this chapter, also write down the stories and family traditions you know about. Do this in narrative style, and for the time being keep your material organized by attaching the narrative to your family group pages.

These activities will get you under way. So far you have made an ancestral chart and some family group pages using the information you have found around the home. You have written down stories and traditions about the family. This is a good start. Now see if you can add a few old photographs to your family history package. Start showing what you are doing to your family and you'll soon see how popular your project is with the relatives. Everyone will want a copy.

Even if you have only a slight interest in family history and genealogy but definitely want to preserve the history of a few generations, you can perform a very worthwhile service by following the advice just given. Type it up neatly, paste in and caption a few old photographs, and make and distribute a few copies. As, or if, you choose to work at research more seriously, you will be exposed to research techniques, records systems, and recording styles that are capable of handling more voluminous data efficiently. For the present, however, you are advised to select easy-to-reach goals. Keep your project simple, but always accurate and neat.

Suggestions for Getting Started

1. If you do not have ready access to such genealogical supplies

as ancestry charts and family group sheet forms, draw an ancestry chart. Make several photocopies of it before filling in information.

2. From your personal knowledge and the personal knowledge of living relatives, combined with information found around the house, fill in the names of your ancestors as far back as you can. Remember to record *maiden* names of maternal ancestors.

3. Using personal knowledge and records around the house, make family group pages for your family and the families of at least the next generation.

4. Write at least two pages of narrative about at least one of the families described on a family group page. See if you can find photographs to help illustrate your story.

5. Begin the above right away. Do not wait until you have completed reading this book.

3
A Total Family
Records System

Family history is literally buried around your house. You must dig it out. This chapter describes how you can incorporate a family records system in your home, and in the process you will find out what family history and genealogy data you already have. Genealogical researchers normally spend many hours in county courthouses and State and Federal archives—records depositories which you will read about in later chapters. One of the most important records depositories, often neglected, is the "home archives." The records in a person's home document the life of that person and of his immediate family. These records, though taken for granted by most, are in fact *the most significant* documents to a person. Sadly, these priceless current papers are usually disorganized and uncontrolled. If your home papers are in such shape, this chapter can change your life. Read it creatively and with enthusiasm!

Happiness is knowing where it is. Following is an excerpt

from a familiar conversation between two members of a typically American family:

> "Where is it? I know it was here yesterday! Mother, where did you put it?"
> "Ask Bobby Jack. I saw him looking at it. You should have put it up."
> "Put it up—where?"

The paperwork explosion that has been affecting government and industry at an accelerating rate during the past generation affects the family as well. The control of the receipt, creation, use, maintenance, retention, protection, and preservation of records is now recognized as an important phase of the management of a home. The fast, efficient, and economical retrieval of information needed by family members *when it is needed* has also made the need for a centralized function of records control increase in importance.

In simpler terms Becky and Bobby Jack can understand, as well as Mother and Dad, "where to put what" needs to be answered quickly. The problem of "where did I put what" needs a quick solution. A simple but sound family records management system can fill these needs. Where to put what *can* be answered quickly. "Where did I put what" *can* become an outdated question for the family records manager.

We have forms, letters, guarantees, warranties, directions, contracts, report cards, insurance policies, records of stock purchases and sales, annual reports, birth certificates, medical claims, bills, newspaper clippings, Richard's poem, Martha's artwork, great-grandmother's informational postcard from Brazil, family history notes, wedding invitations, birth announcements, graduation invitations, thought-provoking articles (that is, things you read and want to keep for future reference), bank statements, budgets, and tax records—to name a goodly number of examples. All of it has a place. And, putting it in place can be easy and fun.

Get Control

For generations people have used and still use the wrong way to get control of the paperwork problem. Here's what happens: You live with a lot of unorganized papers until you die. After you die, your children throw them all away. That's the easy way to get control. Most people take the easy way. A better way is to set up a simple but sound family records management system for use while you are alive and still with your family.

The objectives of a family records management system: I want a place to put things—things that crop up all over—in every room of the house. And, I want to be able to find things when I need them. I want surroundings that are neat and uncluttered. These goals are sound, sensible, and workable. A corollary objective is: When I die, I want to leave my papers in such a way that they can be of value and use to my descendants, other relatives, and friends in documenting the history of my life and that of my family. Some of the things I have collected are priceless, and I don't want everything thrown out when I'm gone.

The getting of control should be gotten now and not left to the children in doing it the easier way. Now is the time to start. We begin by first getting control of our thoughts and attitudes. We must genuinely *want* to have a family records system. Are you ready to stop procrastinating? Do you really want paperwork bliss in your home? O.K. Let's begin.

After you've made up your mind that you are really going to do it, the next step is to find out what you've got. Go through the various boxes, drawers, trunks, and cubby holes around the house and start to inventory your holdings. One idea is to make headings on slips of paper and then stack items under these headings. Make a list of the types of items you find around the house. The list will guide you and will help you add material to the correct piles. Once you have begun to drag things out and have begun to make a list of subjects, you have begun to get *control.*

Get Organized

Filing is the systematic arrangement of records so that they may be quickly found again. In arranging, there are only four ways to classify material: by name, by locality, by subject, and by date. For your family records management system, subject classification is the logical choice. Subject filing is the arranging of material by a given subject; it is filing by descriptive features instead of by name or location.

Under subject classification, one of four arrangements might be chosen: alphabetic, numeric, date, or color. The alphabetic, a basic method of filing, is the logical arrangement choice for our family records system.

There are two types of alphabetic subject files: the dictionary method of many detailed subjects, and the encyclopedic method of a few main headings with many subdivisions. You are advised to use the encyclopedic method.

Find several types of papers that seem to cluster around the same idea. Such as, CERTIFICATES. You may have certificates of birth, school and church accomplishments, vocational training or coursework, graduation, marriage, etc. Or, EXPENSES. You may have papers for many types of expenses: auto, household repair, insurance, medical, utilities, etc. Under FINANCES, you might have subdivisions for such items as bank statements, bonds, budgets, income, mutual funds, loans, stocks, etc.

In many instances you may have second-level subdivisions. Under the FINANCES subject heading, you may create a Taxes subdivision, which could have second-level subdivisions for taxes of the recently-ended year and a separate folder or many folders for taxes for previous years.

In getting *organized*, what you have done is—set up major and minor subject classifications.

A good subject heading must express the topic as exactly and concisely as possible. A single word is best chosen to describe the contents of a folder and that word should be a noun.

Subdivisions must be kept consistent on the level of classification, such as Insurance under the EXPENSES major subject heading. You may have so many insurance papers that you will want to set up Auto, Homeowners, Life, and Medical insurance files as parallel subdivision levels under Insurance.

The subject heading and subdivision headings serve as *addresses* for your papers. The reason a letter can reach you so easily, yet may have begun its journey in a post office hundreds of miles away buried among thousands of items, is due to a few simple classifications. You live in a country, a state, and a city, and you live on a street at a house number. And, of course, you have a name. When you file away your papers, they, too, need an address. The subject headings and appropriate subdivisions give your papers the addresses they need to reach their home in your family records system.

After going through your materials with the intent to group under major subject headings, arrange your subject headings alphabetically. Make an alphabetical list of all your subject headings, and under each subject, list all the subdivisions alphabetically.

Your inventory listing, the result of getting organized, is a guide or index to what is in your paperwork collection. This index provides a quick review of the contents of your file. It particularly helps you choose new subject headings when needed.

Get Filed

Files need not only an address but also a home—file folders and file drawers, file cabinets, or file boxes. Many inexpensive equipment varieties are available today.

Label your folders to match your subject headings and subdivisions. Easy-to-use labels are available, such as the pressure-sensitive self-adhesive folder labels that come mounted on flat sheets of eight labels or on rolls. They can be rolled off the sheet and affixed to the folder tab quickly and neatly without moistening.

File your papers neatly away within the folders in orderly fashion, with the top and left edges even. The letterhead should be at the left side of the drawer. Papers should never hang partially out of a folder. The paper should be folded if it is too large for the folder.

Folders should be kept upright and under compression at all times when the file is not in use to avoid sagging. Folders should not bulge. *It takes eight times longer to file or find a piece of paper in a folder containing 50 pieces than it does in a folder with 10 or less.*

Place and space file guides appropriately throughout your files. Adequate guiding saves human effort and insures accurate and speedy filing and finding. When preparing material to file, segregate papers belonging in different files and prepare cross-references as necessary. Mend torn pages, straighten out crumpled ones, and trim or fold papers too large for folders. Remove all clips and pins. They catch on papers not intended to be fastened together and thus are a fertile source of misfiling. Moreover, they make a file lopsided and hard to handle. Check through every paper even if several are attached, because the grouping may be only a temporary one and the top page may not be the one under which all should be filed.

Use Your File

Calm assurance and peace of mind comes from a functioning family records system. At last your family files are manageable. You know what you've got and where everything is. But, you must *use* your file or there's *no use* having it. As a family merely wanting to keep track of transactions and events, or as a genealogist or historian trying to manage voluminous papers, you are not interested in *files* as such, but only in the *information* that can be obtained *from* your files.

To give effective service, your files must be simple and direct, consistent throughout, expandable for future growth, coordinated to eliminate unnecessary duplications, and purged at regular intervals to eliminate useless papers. Records set up in this manner will provide the family, the genealogist or the historian with a literal *bank* of data that is too complicated to be trusted to memory.

In using your files, that is, enjoying the fruits of your labor in setting up the system, place your file guide (index) at the front of your file to help you use it. When papers start to stack up around the house, it's time to file.

As you use your file, you will occasionally be stumped as to where to file an item. When this happens, you may need to create a new subject heading or a new subdivision. When you do, be sure to add it to your file index.

You can file away items that aren't made of paper, too. The author filed an old watch, mounted on a thin sheet of cardboard, under the subject HISTORY, then under the subdivision for the name of the grandmother who owned it, then under a second subdivision—Artifacts. Because he was there the day they were "throwing things away," the grandson has all of his grandmother's papers incorporated into his family records system under the HISTORY subject classification. Under HISTORY, then under the grandmother's name, then under various subheadings, all of the papers previously contained in six cardboard boxes, now properly organized and filed, are housed in this one storage file drawer. (These folders are housed in a cardboard file *storage* box because they are no longer *active* files.)

The author filed five locks of hair in dated envelopes, gathered from all over the house during the process of setting up his family records system. He filed them under the subject HISTORY, then under the name of the appropriate child. These children's files are thin at first, containing the hospital bracelet and footprint certificate, baby photo, locks of hair, baby congratulation cards, etc. Later, such files expand and subdivide, containing samples of schoolwork, drawings, report cards, and correspondence as the kids grow up. See how everything has a place!

Photographs, too, can be neatly identified and organized in your family records system. One idea is to protect photographs in envelopes within the folders. The envelope prevents photos, especially smaller ones, from sliding out of the ends of the folder.

The important thing to remember is—your files are yours. The system is for you. You will enjoy your family records system more if you will tailor the concept to fit your own family's needs and long-range records preservation and family history and genealogy goals.

Information readily available results in a saving of valuable family time—especially of historical and genealogical research planning and decision-making time. Quickly retrievable information allows for expeditious conduct of research. Well organized files provide a complete history of research performed and a record of communications sent and received.

They won't throw it all away if it's impressively organized and neatly filed. They will be afraid to. Someone will keep it, and because it's properly arranged, your descendants will be able to continue to use and enjoy and praise your collection after you've gone.

Assignment

Set aside a day by yourself. Send everybody else in the family on a picnic. Have a heyday pulling everything out, sorting, stacking, organizing, and filing!

4
The Oral Interview

One of the first things you will want to do is visit older relatives for "oral history" interviews. This is the sophisticated label for talking with them or other individuals to learn what they know about the past. Take the first opportunity to plan such interviews.

Planning

Planning the interview is important. It is wise to think through beforehand the line of questioning that will produce the information you seek. There are several concepts to keep in mind in planning oral history interviews.

Start out by learning all you can in advance about the person to be interviewed. Get information about the personality of the individual: lifestyle, reading habits, hobbies, interests, etc. Knowing this will assist you greatly in the interview. It will especially help you decide ahead of time what you really want to get out of the interview and will help you to plan and prepare a good list of questions.

Your request for an interview will normally be well received. The idea of having information important enough or being someone important enough to be recorded appeals to the ego. Realize the presence of this psychological advantage and use it (but don't abuse it). It is better to make an appointment than to drop in unexpectedly. The opportunity for advance planning is good for the person to be interviewed as well as for the interviewer.

Send the interviewee a list of topics but not specific questions. If the interviewee is furnished a detailed outline, this tends to lead to a stilted interview. Give the person in advance some broad ideas about what you want him to tell you. From then until the interview time, his mind will be turning over things to talk about.

The Questions

There is a danger in using the same line of questioning for different persons. People are different. They cannot be placed in the same mold. The material covered in an interview with a former share-crop farmer will necessarily be dissimilar to that discussed with a former college professor. Both individuals will have interesting, intriguing, and some exciting life stories to relate, but the stories will be couched in entirely different settings. The creative talents of the interviewer will be put to use in designing questions that will draw out the unique personality and the past experiences of each person.

Design questions that will bring out feelings, thoughts about life, and attitudes—ranging from political, to child rearing, to morality and religion. Trades, hobbies, goals, ambitions, and failures as well as successes are significant. Include physical descriptions: color of eyes, hair, complexion, weight, and height. Were they athletic? Were they skilled with tools, resourceful,

38

independent? Any artistic talents? Piano? Painting? If they farmed or ranched as so many did, what were the crops? The stock? How many acres were involved? What kind of soil? How were the water needs met? What kind of dwelling place did they grow up in? What did the rooms look like inside? How many slept in a room? Who slept with whom? Who was the disciplinarian in the family, father or mother? What were the roles of children? Of grandparents? What were the children's duties?

The Interview

The interview will be better if kept informal and conducted in a relaxed atmosphere. The best interviews are on the porch or patio, in the den, or even over lunch or dinner. A good interviewer has to be himself. Don't try to be a Walter Cronkite or a Barbara Walters. Avoid the rapid-fire, news type interview; that is, don't try to play the role of the newsman on the scene of the crime or accident. This is our tendency, however, because we are so exposed to this type of reporting. Newsmen are reporting for display; the family history interview has another purpose. You want to be more conversational than the news reporter. You also want to be more of a listener.

You are there to hear the person talk. Don't anticipate the next answer or introduce a new question instead of listening carefully to the answers to the last question. Think of the interview as directed conversation with the questions serving as guide rails to keep the conversation on the road as it moves along. Too rigid a question plan may not be too successful. An inappropriate question distracts the talker, causing him to switch scenes or topics. Had he not been interrupted, he may have continued his train of thought and provided you with a very good episode or family "tale." And we do want episodes, stories, and family tales, as opposed to a collection of dry facts only.

Do interrupt, however, if you do not understand. Get clarification before going on. Don't let the smallest vagueness go by. Be aware of your role as director of the interview. Keep in mind that questions are the means by which you can change the direction of the interview or can clarify weak or vague points when necessary.

Try to establish early a student-teacher relationship with the other person. As interviewer, you are the student. He is the teacher. Be a good listener, and if he seems tense, throw out a few easy questions—the answers to which he knows and likes to talk about.

There is a tendency for interviewers to try to pick up the jargon and accents of the persons being interviewed, in effect trying to "speak their language." This generally won't work. You are far better off to be yourself.

Today, tape recorders are inexpensive and widely available. Because of this, the "mike fear" once faced by interviewers has somewhat diminished. However, there is a very definite psychological effect caused by the presence of a tape recorder. Fright and often conceit over the whole idea of being interviewed are common reactions. If you encounter fear of a recorder, initiate a chatty conversation before you begin the interview. This may help relax the person. As you chat, casually run a test to see if the equipment is working. The test run will help you set the desired volume level. The test itself is usually enough to eliminate fear and relax the interviewee. Save some tape at the beginning to allow you to go back later and add an official opening statement. This will avoid setting a somewhat formal stage at the beginning and freezing the warm, friendly mood you want to create. Try to get a photograph of the person being interviewed to put on the cover of the transcript you will make later.

Normally 45 minutes to an hour-and-a-half is long enough. If you go much over that amount of time, you will begin to tire your subject. One gets physically tired and mentally tired and cannot remember things as well. At the tiring point, your effectiveness will begin to diminish rapidly. Generally, if you have much ground to cover, it is preferable to plan more than one interview session on different days.

Evaluate the person interviewed as a source of information to help determine the value of the information received. Be alert to exaggerations and possible misrepresentation of facts. When asking for precise detail, such as dates, verification from other sources is advised. Repetition or restatement elsewhere in the interview may provide clues as to accuracy. When dates or names are repeated exactly the same way, this provides a degree of confidence in the accuracy of the interviewee. Notice any bias that may come out of the interview. This, too, is of value.

When your interview is completed, hold a post-mortem on the interview itself. Identify what was done well and what could be improved upon so that you can do an even better job on your next one.

Recording Equipment

Your objective in creating a tape recording of the interview will determine the quality of equipment to be used. If you want to preserve the *voice*, a high quality tape and recorder would produce a more satisfactory and a longer lasting result. *NOTE. Preserved tapes must be played at least every few years to ensure that the taped sounds will not fade out.* If you plan to use the tape only to transcribe the information into written history, the equipment quality is not so important.

If possible, try to place the recording equipment in an inconspicuous location so that it will not command constant attention. This will help ensure a relaxed interview. Avoid the temptation to hide the equipment to get a candid interview. This is unethical, and, if detected, you could lose all access to the person's information.

Don't be overly concerned about background noises. If anything, these sounds reflect the real life setting of the situation.

The tinkling of cups in the background provides a homey atmosphere on the tape. The same applies to background comments, laughter, etc., of other persons who may be present during the interview.

The Transcript

Take the time to make a complete transcription of the interview if at all possible. Prepare it in double-spaced typed copy. Some interviewers prepare verbatim transcripts—noting laughter, sighs, ohs and ahs. Others eliminate nonessential words or comments. Send a copy of your transcript to the person interviewed for his review, commentary, and correction. Then prepare a final transcript. For most family interviews no dispute will arise as to ownership of the tape or of the transcript, but be aware that this can become a legal question, particularly when a public figure or the possibility of libel is involved. Whatever the legalities, always use discretion in dealing with information received from people.

Taking Notes

You can effectively take notes during an interview and not make a recording. In so doing you will try to capture the high points, the essential data, and will necessarily drop out any small talk or fringe information. Another technique is to record part or all of the interview, then later take notes from the tape at your leisure. This is done to avoid the time-consuming task of transcribing a tape.

Brief Visits

Phone calls and brief visits with relatives are mini oral history interviews. Take good notes of these visits also. Record the date and name of the person talked to. Put the information in the file of data you are beginning to accumulate. *Much of the information you are gathering is too valuable to be trusted to memory.*

Remember that for older people, the telephone, especially the long distance telephone, often means trouble or death in the family, so they are not always comfortable with telephone interviews. A personal interview, if at all possible, is preferable.

Suggestions for Your First Interview

1. Select a relative to interview and make an appointment.

2. Decide what you want to accomplish and what kind of information you want to gather.

3. Plan your line of questioning; let it cool, and then go over it two more times on different days.

4. Buy or borrow a tape recorder, become familiar with it, and go to your interview friendly, excited, and unafraid.

5
Your Own Personal History

Most genealogical researchers eventually get so wrapped up in their quest for information about ancestors from the remote past that they overlook or put off doing any compiling and writing about themselves. Although they would love to have had handed down to them a diary or biographical sketch about an ancestor, they are more often than not negligent in leaving such an item for their own posterity. This is a special plea to the beginners in genealogy and family history to plan now to spend an appropriate amount of time and talent in creating a worthy personal history.

This is something you can do entirely at home. Your "research" will be among the documents in your own private archives at home. All the paperwork and memorabilia around the house, the photograph albums, the letters, the certificates, diaries, keepsakes, etc., document your life and are there to help you remember and to give you ideas on what to write.

The hardest part of writing a personal history is getting

started. To overcome that, at the first opportunity after you read this, take out a pad of lined paper and put a pen in your hand. Write the words "I was born" and then continue. Don't pay close attention at all to what or how you say whatever rolls forth out of your head onto the paper. Analyzing, evaluating, editing, adding to, crossing out, and changing can all come later. The main thing is to get under way.

Once you have begun to write, as you think of things and write them down, these remembered events will stimulate your memory and you will recall other things to write about. I am firmly convinced that we have the built-in capability of literally remembering everything that ever happened to us. The trick is to trigger the memory and make it work for us. It is not necessary to write down all you remember. That would take too many volumes to record. You do want to remember the highlights, the significant, the meaningful, the things that affected, molded, directed, and motivated your life—the people involved, the work, and the moving, loving, life-giving experiences that made you who and what you are.

It is easier to approach the job bite-size by breaking it down. Concentrate first on your early years. Call this section your "early life" or your "childhood years." Dig out all the photographs and keepsake items you have that relate to your life from birth to about 12 years. If your parents are living, you will need to pay them a visit to see what they have tucked away that relates to you.

Type up your handwritten draft and leave some space to add photographs to the typescript. Type captions under the photographs you include. You will become excited as you see the documented story of your life begin to take shape. Don't number the pages yet, and try to end episodes near the bottom of a page. As you think of additions, type up the added page and insert it where it chronologically belongs. Later, when you feel like you have thought about everything, or your modesty signals it is time to close that section, you can add the page numbers. Continue writing in this fashion, moving into the other stages of your life one at a time, i.e. youth, college years, adult life, and retirement. You don't have to wait until retirement to start writing. I am encouraging my children to write about their childhood years as soon as they complete them and begin to embark upon the teenage stage.

Talk about your personality, your quirks, your talents, your likes and dislikes. State opinions. Be honest in sizing yourself up. Be fair in dealing with your mistakes. But don't write a "dirty book," that is, don't be overly candid in describing any immorality or sordid events that you may have experienced. If you had problems, were divorced, fired from a job, or the like, there is a tactful, objective way to say so. It may even help you emotionally to bring the information out and put it in writing, and the doing of it may be educational for your children in helping them avoid similar mistakes. It will make you "human."

Don't be modest, either. If you are productive, creative, or a genius in some way or in many ways, tell it. State the facts. If you are a plain Jane or Bill, or think you are, don't worry that you have not traveled down the Amazon or made a million in the stock market. Most of the people in the world are like you, yet each is an interesting, unique person with a story to tell. Just try hard to paint as true a picture of yourself as possible.

What do you do with your personal history once you have written it? Make a few photocopies (Xerox or other brand). The copying machines are now developed to the point where you will even get fairly good reproductions of the photographs you include. Give copies of your personal history to your parents, your brothers and sisters, and to your children. Keep your master copy in a safe place at home. Add to it from time to time as you remember things from the past, and as new events transpire in your life. In some localities, the public libraries or historical or genealogical societies have programs underway to collect and preserve such histories. If you discover such a program, be sure to donate a copy of your personal history. Your work may be included in a book someday, one you may later create or possibly one a descendant will produce a hundred years from now.

Start Writing Right Away

1. Sit down with a lined pad and a pen and start writing whatever pops into your head about your childhood.

2. Make yourself keep writing until you have turned out at least a half dozen handwritten pages. Then write more on subsequent days.

3. Go through the house, or your parents' house, and pull together a collection of pictures that depict your childhood.

4. Be creative and imaginative in continuing to produce your own personal history. Be kind to yourself and allow plenty of time to do it, but not so much that you wind up never completing it.

6
The Slide/Tape Program

One of the most exciting, entertaining, and worthwhile developments in the family history field is the slide/tape program on families or on specific family members. Many families today own or have access to cameras capable of producing slides, and the cassette tape recorder is in nearly every home. This equipment is being used to create wonderful programs for relaying the family history to the younger generations.

Here's what people are doing. They are making slides from old photographs. They are adding to this collection of slides more slides taken of places, people, and things connected with the life of the person or family being featured. They are recording the voices of the people being featured. These tapes will be played while the slides are shown. If the featured individual is deceased, they are recording the children, grandchildren, other relatives, and friends of the person featured, as these people tell what they know about that person.

What is the result? A very moving, touching, heartwarming

family story—that comes to life as you see it on the screen and as you listen to the voices of the persons who experienced the story or who were at least a part of it. How much more penetrating when appropriate music is in the background, or is used for effect—like the movie people use it.

Here are some ideas of things you can do. First, decide on a person to feature in your first attempt at a slide/tape program. Perhaps you have selected your mother. She is still living but advanced in years, and you want her to share the fun of a special show just about her. Round up a good collection of early photographs in which she appears. Go right on back to her childhood if you can and bring her up to date. Span her entire life with photographs.

As you search for photographs, be on the alert for artifacts and keepsakes to photograph. Her baby clothes, her wedding dress, the first quilt she made, a spelling award, a clipping telling of her being made PTA president—you will find a number of things that will help tell "her story."

Take a trip to the places where she lived, and take slides of the house, the farm, the church, the stores she shopped in, the school she attended. Photograph her living friends and relatives, particularly those she loved the most and spent the most time with.

Think of things to photograph as you "interview" her on tape (see the separate chapter on interviewing). Make notes or add to your idea list as she talks. Bring out photographs or things to help jog her memory. "Mother, where were you living when this was taken?" "Whose old car was that you were sitting on?" "Were you visiting the coast when this was made, or did you live near there at one time?"

You can visit national, state, and local archives and historical societies to pick up ideas for more slides that will enliven your presentation. Suppose her husband was in World War I, and he had to leave her at home soon after marriage. You could make a slide of a World War I recruiting poster at the National Archives.

And you could find there recorded World War I era music that you could copy. This would be perfect to "dub in" while you show slides of the recruiting poster, of Papa in his uniform, and slides of scenes of the devastation Papa witnessed. Remember, though, you are featuring Mama, but events in Papa's life are inseparably entwined with hers.

Mama made it through the Great Depression. The depositories have many materials describing and illustrating these historic years. Use these general historical items and intersperse them with the specific slides of mother and the family. This will help recreate a history of the family not only at home but in society. Your work will become family history in every sense of the word as you weave social history in with the family story.

A good practice is to make a list of the major social events that occurred during the person's lifetime. Then think of things that you could research out that would help illustrate these events. Also, list the sounds, music, and voices you could record that would help give an added dimension to your program. Think of such things as recording the almost silence of a day on the farm, disturbed only by the breeze and the rubbing, crying sounds of the turning of a windmill. Splice in that strip of tape for a pause when you show a slide of the old farm, or of the remains of that old windmill.

Suggestions

1. Pay close attention to the next slide/sound presentations you may see at school, work, or church. Note the techniques used, and try to get ideas for a family slide/tape program.

2. Try a simple slide/tape program right away, using what you have readily available. Further develop your skills as you gain access to more materials, and eventually create several good programs about your family to preserve for posterity.

7
Try To Find Interested Distant Relatives

Chances are good that unknown distant relatives are working on your ancestral lines. Your problem is to learn of their work. To share information with them is to avoid duplication of effort—try to find them!

When you are visiting relatives, ask if anyone else in the family has ever done any work on the family tree. More often than not someone in the family has already laid the groundwork for you. You may even discover that a close relative has long had a keen interest in the family and has collected a lot of information. Contact anyone mentioned as a possible source of information. Do it as soon as possible.

You can explore for distant relatives through the use of genealogical societies. First find out if there is a local genealogical society. Many cities and counties have them. There are also regional and state societies. Quite often local genealogical societies hold their meetings in public libraries, and they sometimes deposit genealogical books and periodicals in the local library as a supportive effort. Your local librarian can usually tell you how to contact the group which can be most helpful to you.

Most genealogical clubs and societies publish regular (usually quarterly) newsletters or magazines. Within these periodicals there is usually a "query" section. These sections are popular parts of these publications. In the query sections, members or subscribers place brief advertisements, known as queries, wherein they mention the surnames and localities in which they have an interest. People who see a query and who are working on that same family in that place then write to the person who placed the query.

An example of a query is: "ROGERS, Morgan Co., Ala., 1800s." This tells the reader you have research in process for members of the Rogers family who lived in Morgan County, Alabama, during the 1800s. This is sufficient information to get you in touch with others who are concentrating on the Rogers family in that place at that time. In the letters that researchers exchange following the publication of the query, more detailed information can be shared. Full names, dates, and abstracts of information from documents can be exchanged through the mails. It is not necessary to exchange the detail in the genealogical periodical. Detailed queries (and many people place them) only serve to clutter periodicals.

The most widely circulated genealogical magazine is *The Genealogical Helper*. This magazine was started many years ago with the goal of helping people who are working on the same families to get together. The *Helper* has been successful in accomplishing its goal. Today, the magazine also publishes helpful articles about research in specific areas. Its pages also provide advertisements of publishers, announcements of new books, availability of supplies, names of professional researchers, and family associations, as well as thousands of listed exchange queries. There is a charge for subscribers to have a query published.

Carefully consider how the query procedure might benefit

you. Assume you have exhausted home sources, and you have added to your data by visiting living relatives. You have found that your ancestor Reuben Taylor lived in Rankin County, Mississippi, before moving to Texas in about 1870. You would like to write to other people who are interested in your Rankin County Taylor family. Go to the largest public library near you. See if the library has a genealogical collection. Does it have any genealogical periodicals? Is there a local genealogical society? Does the library have *The Genealogical Helper?* Does the library possibly receive state or regional genealogical publications? If you are lucky, you will find back issues to browse through. Look at these for Taylor queries. If you don't have local access to genealogical materials, you may wish to subscribe to the *Helper* or other magazines. When you have finished using your copies, you could donate the magazines to the library to help it begin to build a collection of genealogical items.

As soon as possible you should place a query in *The Genealogical Helper* (Everton Publishers, P.O. Box 368, Logan, Utah 84321) and any existing regional, state, or local publications. The style might be as follows or perhaps a style recommended by the editor of the magazine:

TAYLOR, Rankin Co., Miss., 1800s (followed by your name and address)

Don't forget to find out if there is a county genealogical society in existence in the county of your research problem. Suppose your research involved the Lee family of Johnston County, North Carolina. You could join the Johnston County Genealogical Society and receive its quarterly publication. Through it you would discover other Lee researchers and you would learn that there is a wealth of Johnston County Lee material in the Johnston County Room in the library located in the county seat at Smithfield. You would find that many distant relatives have been working on the Lee family for years and have attempted to "turn over all the stones" in the courthouse and elsewhere in the Lee ancestry quest.

Suggestions for Getting in Touch with Distant Relatives

1. Visit the largest public library near you. Find out: a) if there is a local genealogy club or society you can join, b) if there is a genealogical collection at the library, and c) whether the library subscribes to *The Genealogical Helper* or other periodicals that interest you.

2. Place a genealogical query in a coming issue of *The Genealogical Helper.*

3. Place a genealogical query in a forthcoming issue of a genealogical magazine which specializes in the state or region covering the area of your research problem. (There is either a state society or a genealogical magazine for most states.)

4. Place a genealogical query in the *Journal of Genealogy*, Robert D. Anderson Publishing Co., 150 South 38th St., Omaha, NE 68131. This is a relatively new magazine, published *monthly.*

5. Place a genealogical query in the *weekly* genealogical magazine, *Family Puzzlers*, published by Heritage Papers, Danielsville, GA 30633.

6. While waiting for responses from your own ads, start writing to people who have placed queries in past magazines if they seem to relate to the families in which you have an interest.

8
Writing To Relatives

Writing and getting letters is one of the most enjoyable aspects of tracing your family. It can be like Christmas when the mail brings needed names and dates. The wider you cast your net—that is, the more letters you write—the more bountiful the catch!

Keep letters friendly and genealogically to the point. Always write legibly, or type letters if possible. It is wise to set forth your genealogical question clearly. You might even restate the question on a separate sheet at the end of the letter. This helps remind the reader that an answer is needed.

A cardinal rule for beginners in letter writing is *never ask someone to send you a copy of all they have on a family*. It is important not to ask for too much at one time. It is better to keep brief answers flowing back to you rather than risk overwhelming the reader with too many questions at once. If you choke the reader with a series of whopper questions, he will frequently put your letter aside until he has more time to answer it. *The letter may never surface again.* If you ask a veteran genealogist for a copy of all he has on a family, you can be sure your request will be received with a laugh. He may well have a whole file drawer of information on that one family. Thus, to comply with your request would be an impossible task.

When requesting information from a correspondent, always record the date and your address on the letter as well as on the envelope. Be sure to include your postal zip code. Also, enter an inside address of the person to whom you are writing. It is best to make a carbon copy of the letter. At least keep a record of the name of the person, the date, and a record of information sent and/or requested. The carbon copy or letter record is not so important at the time you write the letter because the information you need is fresh on your mind. The importance of the copy emerges later when you are coming back to a problem that you have set aside for awhile.

In a later chapter your genealogical files will be discussed. You will be advised to keep information filed by surname. When writing letters that cover more than one family, it is helpful to put the information or the questions about each family on separate sheets. Your carbon copies of correspondence can then be separately filed in the appropriate surname files.

A practice has developed among genealogical letter writers to include in outgoing letters a self-addressed stamped envelope (s.a.s.e.). In fact, postage has become such an expense that some people do not answer letters when a s.a.s.e. is not enclosed. Try to remember always to enclose one, or at least enclose return postage. Use a business-letter size envelope for your s.a.s.e. The person at the other end may want to send you material that would be awkward to fold down into a small envelope.

As you would do with any letter written to request a favor, always keep its tone and manner courteous. The person to whom you write has no obligation to help you. Also, if you are in a position to do it, and think it may be welcome, offer to supply information on your own family or branch of the family in

question. You want to give as well as to receive help by correspondence.

Suggestions for Writing Productive Letters

1. Pinpoint one or a few items of information you are missing,
   such as dates of birth, marriage, or death, which you have
   reason to think a relative might know.

2. Write a friendly letter to the relative, and in the body of the
   letter mention that you have become interested in the family
   genealogy. Say that you need certain information and that
   you will list it on a separate page.

3. Itemize on a separate sheet to enclose with your letter *no more
   than three* questions. Make a carbon copy of your letter for
   your files.

4. Enclose a self-addressed stamped envelope (business letter
   size, folded) and rush to the post office. When you get home
   from the post office, write to somebody else while you are
   waiting for an answer to your first letter!

9
The Family Research Club Or Organization

Now that you have found others who are just as interested in your family as you are, you can get organized—in unity there is strength—and form a research club or family organization. You can start with as few as two or three people. Here's what you and a group can do and how it will help you.

First, select *one* family surname to organize around. You may want to organize the research on other surnames, too, but at the beginning select just one. List the names and addresses of all your close relatives interested in that surname, and include all the new distant relatives you have discovered. (Remember—you learned about the distant relatives when you advertised your interests in that family by placing queries in *The Genealogical Helper* and other genealogical periodicals. If you haven't done that yet—do it!)

If many of these people live close by, your next step is to call a meeting in your home. If the people you have discovered are scattered from Falls Church, Virginia, to San Diego, California, omit the meeting and start writing letters. Either way, you and your relatives and new related friends should decide on a plan of action.

At this point, how you go about organizing and the selection of officers are minor considerations. The foremost action items are to get together (or in touch) with at least one or two others, decide what you are going to do, write it down, divide up the work, and then *go to work*.

Once your research team has started work, you have planted the seed for an eventual "going" organization. Now that you are under way, as you discuss plans and actually work with fellow team members, you'll find that ideas snowball. Officers, dues, a quarterly newsletter, a family reunion—all of these will come in due time. Over a period of months or years, your official family organization will emerge.

The family organization generally has as its major goal the compiling and recording of genealogical and historical information pertaining to the common ancestors of its members. Cooperation in genealogical research through the family organization is one of the most successful means of extending and proving pedigrees and compiling family genealogies. The family organization promotes coordination of research among individuals researching the same family lines, affords opportunities for specialization in research, pools time and money resources, channels wise use of resources, and fosters fellowship and understanding among its members. Frequent association with other members in family organizations, through both personal contact and correspondence, brings definite feelings of concern for family and greater appreciation of family ties. By working with others of the group, each member becomes family oriented and feels he is part of a big family operation.

The family organization or research team specializing in one surname is a sound, logical way to solve "dead-end" problems. The Taylors, the Barlows, the Williamses, the Stephenses, the Hayneses, the Stewarts, the Newtons, the Murphrees, the Kilgores, and many others, have such groups underway. These are united efforts to squeeze out of the existing available records all the genealogical data pertaining to a given family. Within a relatively short time, a cooperating group of researchers is able to become the research center for the family. Usually, central files are established and indexes and cross-reference files are made. Cooperation is the byword. Free sharing and exchange of information is the order of the day. The genealogical community benefits greatly from these groups. Everyone does. So will you. And you will have fun, too.

Getting Started

Many members of the Locke family, descendants of Thomas Locke of Virginia, who migrated westward, are living in Missouri. Bryan Locke, a young man from Jefferson City, Missouri, for several months sought correspondents to find out more about the Locke family and to meet some of his Locke relatives. He compiled a card file of names and addresses of over 100 living persons to whom he was related. Bryan discovered that about 20 of these were very interested in the family. The family organization plan seemed very logical to Bryan, and since he had discovered no such organization already in existence, a special meeting was called to organize. To set up the special meeting, Bryan sent detailed letters to the 20 vitally interested persons, outlining the advantages of organizing. He mentioned some possible goals the organization could set and his ideas for a sound organization structure. When all the arrangements were made, all the persons whose names appeared in the file of addresses were invited to the meeting. Twenty-six persons attended the special meeting, and a fully organized Thomas Locke Family Organization was the result.

(*Note.* Fictitious example).

Several descendants of the Wimberly family of early Georgia were in frequent communication by mail, informing one another

of family activities and assisting each other in Wimberly genealogical research. These individuals were widely scattered geo-
graphically—two living in Texas, one in California, several in
Georgia and Florida, and one each in Idaho and Washington.
Occasionally other individuals from various areas would join in
the correspondence. The idea was put forth to organize the
Wimberly family. Among themselves and by mail, these corresponding individuals agreed on appointments to fill the offices
that all felt were necessary. An efficient Wimberly Family Organization was soon in operation. With the pooling of effort and
wise use of resources, the organization rapidly gained momentum
and membership. Within a few months, the organization boasted
a membership of 75, with a quarterly family publication keeping
the members interested and informed, and yet *none of the officers
had ever met*!

(*Note.* Fictitious example).

The Work

The family research club or organization members go to work at
gathering in genealogical data. With many working, much more
information can be found in depositories. More letters can be
written with the aim to stimulate the digging out of data from
the various family trunks and attics around the country. Specific
assignments to search certain censuses, courthouses, cemeteries,
etc., can be made as the work is supervised and coordinated. This
participation—involving as many family members as possible in
activities and research projects—is one of the most important
ingredients for success.

The organization pulls together early photographs of common ancestors. It collects stories about the family, writes down
family traditions, and creates oral history tape recorded interviews of family members. Family antiques and artifacts still in
existence are cataloged, photographed, displayed, and sometimes

placed for safekeeping with interested local museums or historical societies.

Files and indexes are created. Books, papers, and magazines or newsletters are published. Reunions and conventions are sponsored.

Finance through Newsletter Subscriptions

To finance the work, dues or subscription fees for the newsletter or magazine can be collected. This is the way the Newton Research Club operates. Over a hundred people work together. They pay dues to one person, Mrs. Wilda Newton Page of Fritch, Texas, who houses the Newton central files. By excerpting interesting bits and pieces from the correspondence she receives from club members, Mrs. Page puts out a newsy, helpful quarterly research club newsletter.

The Linder Family Association is funded by subscriptions to *The Linder Quarterly*. The association's secretary has thousands of Linders cataloged on family group record forms housed in a number of heavy-duty 3-ring binders. These are fully indexed on 3 x 5 cards. The secretary is also editor of the *Quarterly*, which highlights the happenings of modern day Linder families—Linders in politics, science, religion, movies, business, car racing, you name it; Linders getting married, having babies, graduating, dying—as well as Linders in history. Most appreciated by the subscribing Linders around the country are the photographs published in the *Quarterly*. This sharing of old family photographs made possible by the quarterly magazine is one of the principal services the organization provides the members.

The Murphree Genealogical Association finances with a combination-type subscription plan which appeals to the generosity, level of interest in history, and financial capability of the members. It offers a $5 "subscription," a $10 "active membership," and a $15 (or more) category for "Murphree Research

Club" members. With some 20 or more persons contributing $15 or better and another 10 to 20 contributing $10, more funds are available to finance the association activities.

Special fund-raising activities that churches, PTAs and civic organizations get into are also successfully adapted to family organizations. Why not auction off a framed hand-painted family coat-of-arms, family quilt, or a dozen cakes made from family recipes at the next family reunion!

Publications

The most important publication of the family organization is the quarterly family magazine or newsletter. Why quarterly? Monthly is too often. Nobody has time to work on it that frequently. Every six months or once a year is not enough to keep the needed communication going.

A family book can be a long-range goal. Books cost and take time. However, with many working and combining talents and resources, the family organization is perhaps the best vehicle for publishing family books.

Reunions/Conventions

For close-knit families where everybody knows everybody else, the get-together is a "reunion." When the research club was formed by mail and the members have never before met, it's a "convention."

Whichever, the meeting should be planned for fun. Fun is the main ingredient. Everyone needs to have a good time. Since not everyone enjoys the same things, diversity in the program planning is a must. Plan to eat well, to sing, to dance (yes, dance—even to rock music because you will *bring your young people to the reunion!*), and to play games. When planning the family reunion or convention, the committee (and the committee should be absolutely loaded with people, lots of people) should ask itself this question: "What can we do to make sure that everybody present has one of the most enjoyable experiences of his lifetime?"

Avoid being too businesslike with the program. Have business, yes, but take care of it in a friendly, informal way, moderately businesslike but not in a strict, stilted "Roberts Rules of Order" fashion. Much of the family business can be handled beforehand by committee and merely presented and hurriedly voted upon at the general convocation. Be advised that not everyone in the family is interested in history. Many will be present to visit only, and not to hear "endless genealogies."

Pick a good park or picnic area as a site. One national family organization meets in different tourist cities in the United States. Another mixes tourist sites with family towns. Holding national conventions every third year, the latter held its first convention in 1967 in Colorado Springs; in 1970 in Gatlinburg, Tennessee; in 1973 in a family town in Missouri; and in 1976 in Spartanburg, South Carolina, an area where family members had resided for nearly 150 years.

In July 1970 the Murphree Genealogical Association held its first national convention in Murfreesboro, North Carolina. My family attended. As we drove into this ancient little town that is now busily engaged in restoration projects, we were pleasantly shocked to see a wide banner across the main street saying "Welcome Murphrees." When we parked the car to make a drugstore purchase, another surprise. In every store window in town "Welcome Murphrees" posters were displayed, containing a reproduced portrait of the Revolutionary War hero Hardy Murfree, son of the town's founder, William Murfree. We were in for more pleasant surprises. A bus tour of the town, proudly showing off the restorations, including the mayor's restored 18th century "Melrose Plantation" home, the original home of William Murfree, and a reception there with all the town gentry present. It was hot out in the yard that day. I wondered how many generations before me had commented on the heat at such receptions in that yard—all the way back to long hoop skirts and white plantation suitery.

A cousin proudly thrust before me a folded newspaper. In it was a detailed article about the Murfree family. *The Herald* had published it the day before we arrived: "As Welcome to Visitors, Murfree Family History Recounted," prepared by Dr. Tom Parramore of Raleigh, professor of history at Meredith College and historian of note.

We had a business meeting and election of new officers, and a full catered banquet, with entertainment and a few short, humorous but appropriate speeches. The banquet was also attended by state political figures and the press.

For my family the most memorable part was the fun and camaradarie we had at the dorms at Chowan College where we were housed. The kids tossed coins to see who got to be grandmother's roommate; we had three dormitory rooms. The presence in the halls of a New York comedienne-actress—(you mean she's our cousin!)—kept us in stitches while sitting around the dorm lounge area. There was a piano, and soon we had our own "gospel chorus" in concert. That weekend there was a fresh breeze of wholesome goodness blowing in that little northeastern North Carolina town of Murfreesboro.

Secrets of Success[1]

Participation.   Involve as many family members as possible in activities and research projects.

Services.   Provide definite and worthwhile services for contributing members.

1. From tabulating the results of a 1965 survey conducted by the author, in which all known U.S. family genealogy associations, reunion associations, family history groups, etc., were contacted.

Communications.   Establish active communications through a quarterly family periodical.

Leadership.   Acquire youth, enthusiasm for family history, and leadership qualities in leadership positions.

Suggestions

1.   Try to find a family organization already in existence on one of your family lines. Join it, and offer to accept a work assignment.

2.   Get together with relatives and organize a family reunion.

3.   Give it some thought, then move into action and set into motion a family research club or organization.

part two

Your Adventure In The Public Records And In The Libraries

10
An Overview Of Sources Available To You

Have you exhausted all home sources? Have you gleaned all you can from close relatives? Have you collected information from gravestones in all nearby cemeteries? Have you contacted others working on the family genealogy? If your answers are "yes," your next question is "Where do I go now?" You will proceed to the records of public depositories: libraries, historical and genealogical societies, county courthouses, and state and national archives.

Remember, research can be performed wherever you find records of your ancestors preserved. Beginning researchers are surprised to learn of the many records that were created and are still available. What one must do is think of what records might have been created involving an ancestor during his lifetime, then try to find those records. It's simple. Try it. Regrettably, sometimes needed records that were created in the past do not remain today. But, those that do remain can often provide the answers to the questions you have about the family.

With the exception of New England States and a few other scattered areas, the procedure of recording births and deaths officially began generally in this country during the period 1850-1920. Marriage records often begin much earlier. In practice, however, in the early years many births and deaths, especially in rural areas, were never officially recorded with the appropriate agencies.

Before official state birth and death registration were required, the only place such information was regularly recorded was in church registers and family bibles. Of course, some churches did not usually record such data. For example, Baptist church records reflect the acceptances and dismissals of members but seldom any vital data. The author found in Baptist records that his ancestor was put out of the church for his "excessive use of spiritous liquors" but the records gave no insight as to his dates of birth, death, or marriage. On the other hand, Episcopal, Catholic, Quaker, and other church records are rich in genealogical data. Your job will be to learn if these records have been preserved and then to search for the information they may contain about your family.

In the county courthouses of most states you will find all official county records, such as land and other property transfers, estate records, court action papers, and marriage records. These often yield valuable genealogical data. Many of the county records have been microfilmed and are available in locations other than the county courthouse. The counties may also have tax lists, guardians' records and many others, all of which may be quite informative in shedding light on your ancestors' lives. Careful reading of all county records may even supply birth or death dates, or at least enable you to approximate them.

The federal government started taking censuses in 1790. One of the first things you will do is consult the 1900 federal census to find your ancestors living that year. After finding them in 1900, you will proceed backward through each available decennial census finding your ancestors and copying the entries into your records files. Many states also took separate censuses, and some, such as the New York State census of 1855, may be of very great importance to your search.

The federal and state governments have also created military service records and other records relating to military service. The granting of pensions and bounty land for military service was documented in such records. The federal records are available to you through the National Archives in Washington. Some of these records are also available through the regional branches of the National Archives located in various metropolitan areas throughout the country. State records are in state archives, such as records of pensions granted by some Confederate states.

There are other types of records available for particular localities during certain time periods, many of which will be discussed fully later. What is important to know at this introductory stage is that a great many research sources will be available to you; that these records were for the most part created by governmental bodies; and that they are generally preserved by the historical and archival agents of these bodies. You will need to learn of the extant records relating to your problems and their locations.

Individuals and organizations have created many useful compiled sources in the form of published books which can greatly aid your search. You will find published family genealogies, county histories, and abstracts and indexes of various series of records in libraries, in historical and genealogical societies, and in some archives.

Recommended Reading

At your public library, scan or "pre-read" (that is, look at the cover, read the preface and contents pages, and thumb through the book, noting chapter and subsection headings, and start to absorb an overview of the contents) Val D. Greenwood's *The Researcher's Guide to American Genealogy* (Baltimore: Genealogical Publishing Co., 1975), and *Genealogical Research: Methods and Sources*, volumes 1 (Washington, 1960) and 2 (Washington, 1971), published by the American Society of Genealogists.

11
The Research
Sources

The general guideline is: Look wherever there were records kept that might relate to your ancestors. You never know where or when they may have been involved in recorded transactions. Some of the places their names will show up will surprise you. We normally look first for records of them in the areas where they lived. Our task is thus to learn about all the records that exist for an area in a time period. We need to become familiar with the records created at all levels of government—national, state, and local.

The National Archives

Although the National Archives was not established until the mid-1930s, its holdings date back to Revolutionary War times. They capture the sweep of the past from that time forward. The National Archives is the nation's official depository for records created by the federal government and deemed to have lasting historical value. Literally millions of records relating to persons who have had dealings with the government are on deposit.

The National Archives was created primarily for use by the government, but its rich stores of material are available to all. As a matter of policy the Archives does not perform research for the public, but it does make the records freely available. As will be discussed later, the National Archives can provide photocopies of records for a fee when the inquirer can adequately identify the needed information so that the staff can readily find what is wanted among the vast holdings.

The Federal Census

The most widely used record ever created by the government is the federal census of population. The first census was taken in 1790 for the purpose of apportioning representation to Congress. A population census has been taken every ten years since that time.

The National Archives has the 1790-1870 originals, a microfilm copy of the 1880 census, the surviving fragments of the 1890 census, and a microfilm copy of the 1900 census. Later censuses are under restriction and have not been released for public use. Unless legislation is passed or regulations created to the contrary, the 1910 census will probably be released for public use in 1985, when it becomes age 75. Recent censuses are withheld from researchers out of respect to the privacy of living individuals who were enumerated.

The 1790-1840 censuses give the names of the free heads of household only; other family members are tallied by age and sex but are not named. In 1850 a very great decision was made—at least for the field of genealogy. That year the census takers listed the names and ages of every free person living in every household. Also listed was the state, territory, or country of birth of each free person. Additional information was included with each succeeding census.

The census records are one of the first records a beginning searcher should seek out. Through their use, families of ancestors living during the period 1850-1900 can be entirely or partially reconstituted, while the 1790-1840 censuses may provide very good leads and circumstantial data that will help solve genealogical problems.

One of the tremendous things about census records is their unequaled availability. All of the census records available at the National Archives have been microfilmed, and copies of the microfilm have been widely purchased. Many state and local historical and genealogical societies, large public libraries, and state and university libraries and archives have purchased microfilm copies of census records.

A good practice is to find out from your new friends (the ones you have made who are doing genealogical research), or from your local library or genealogical society, what census holdings may be available to you right in your area.

Some state libraries will loan their census microfilm via interlibrary loan to your local library. The regional archives branches of the National Archives have complete sets of census microfilm, 1790-1900, and the regional archives also loan census microfilm via interlibrary loan. If there is near you a branch genealogical library of the vast Genealogical Society Library, you can have film sent out from Salt Lake City. Or, if you don't like one of those options, you can buy outright from the National Archives your own microfilm copies of census records.

A list of the regional branches of the National Archives, with hours, addresses, and phone numbers can be obtained by writing to : Correspondence Branch, National Archives, Washington, DC 20408. To find out if there is a branch of the Salt Lake City facility near you, write to: Branch Genealogical Libraries, The Genealogical Society, 50 East North Temple St., Salt Lake City, Utah 84150. Ask for the name, street address, telephone number, and hours of the library nearest your city of residence. (These branch libraries are further discussed in the chapter on "Genealogical Libraries."

Federal Military Service and Related Records

You can fill out a government form and send it to Washington and for a nominal charge you will be supplied with photocopies of the documents the National Archives has on your ancestor who fought in any of the early wars. The files begin with the Revolutionary War. The records of men who fought in the Revolutionary War are not complete as there were two fires that caused some losses. An office fire in 1800 was followed by more fire losses when the British burned Washington during the War of 1812. Nonetheless the National Archives has a good collection of Revolutionary War records and fairly complete records of the other early wars.

There are files at the National Archives on men who fought in all the wars up to World War I. The records on men who fought in World War I and later wars are at the National Military Personnel Records Center (MPRC), GSA, 9700 Page Blvd., St. Louis, MO 63132. Requests for records housed at the National Personnel Records Center should be made on Standard Form 180, Request Pertaining to Military Personnel Records.

One type of record available is the compiled military service record. These compiled service records are just what the name implies. They are files that include data compiled from various records created during a soldier's service. It must be remembered that in the early days detailed records were not made as they are today. Using what records were available, the War Department made compilations of soldiers' service information before the records themselves were retired to the National Archives. Employees went through muster rolls, pay rolls, hospital lists, prisoner lists, etc., and abstracted the information onto cards.

The various cards for a soldier were sorted into file jackets. Normally there is not in the files much personal data about a soldier or his family. Often you find his age at enlistment and the place of enlistment, which can be valuable information. Occasionally a death date is in the file, particularly when the soldier died in service.

Pension application files are the most valuable records relating to military service. These files often are rich in genealogical data. The most valuable pension files are those that involve a widow receiving a pension. In order to start receiving the pension, the widow had to prove she married the soldier. It is normal to find in the files the marriage date and place, the name of the minister who performed the ceremony, the maiden name of the wife, and often other good information. Sometimes pages from the family bible were sent to Washington as the only available written proof of marriage or age. These old family bible pages are still in many of the pension application files.

Before 1855 the government gave away bounty land for military service. The bounty land warrant application files also often contain information of genealogical value. Normally you at least find the veteran's age at the time of application and his then current county and state of residence, both of which are good genealogical information.

Whenever you know an ancestor fought in one of the early wars, or even if you only suspect he did, it is essential to order copies of the available files that may relate to his service, any pension he or his heirs may have received, or any available bounty land application relating to the service. Ordering copies of veteran's records has been made easy. You fill out GSA Form 6751, Order and Billing for Copies of Veteran's Records. Minimum identifying data required are the veteran's name, the war, and the state he served from. Blank forms are available by writing to: Correspondence Branch, National Archives, Washington, DC 20408.

Passenger Arrival Records

The passenger arrival records in the National Archives list names of passengers who arrived at ports on the Atlantic Ocean or in the Gulf of Mexico and a few inland ports. The available records consist of passenger lists, transcripts, abstracts, baggage lists, and manifests.

Although there are lists for as early as 1798, most of them are for the years 1820-1945, and for those years there are many gaps. The lists dated before 1819 are primarily baggage lists that are a part of the cargo manifests.

The San Francisco passenger lists were destroyed by fires in 1851 and 1940, and lists for other Pacific coast ports, if they exist, have not been transferred to the National Archives. During the 19th century the law did not require passenger arrivals records as such to be kept for persons entering the United States by land from Canada and Mexico.

Whereas thousands came during the Colonial period, for which the National Archives has no holdings, it was later that the great tidal wave of migration hit the Atlantic Coast of this country. A great bulk of immigrants came during the 100-year period 1815-1914. Some 35 million Europeans immigrated during this period, most of whom came through the Port of New York. Although the passenger arrival records in the National Archives are incomplete, the available lists document a high percentage of 19th century immigration. The voluminous lists are handwritten and are chronologically arranged by port.

The lists consist mainly of customs passenger lists and immigration passenger lists. Customs and immigration passenger lists were received by the collectors of customs and later by the immigration officials at the ports of arrival from the captains or masters of vessels. This was done in compliance with federal law.

There are some indices to the passenger arrival records but the indices are not complete. The National Archives will consult an index for you and if the name of your ancestor is found will make a photocopy of the corresponding passenger list for a nominal charge. This service can be obtained by use of GSA Form 7111, Order and Billing for Copies of Passenger Lists. In some cases, in order for the staff to find the list, you must provide the very information you want to know. However, in a great many instances the staff is able to locate lists with a minimum of data supplied by you. Order blank forms from: Correspondence Branch, National Archives, Washington, DC 20408.

When you write for forms, ask for free leaflets and any other forms or informational materials that will help you use the National Archives for genealogical purposes. These items will introduce you to other records of genealogical value in the National Archives. The three "high-volume" records used most are those mentioned above—census, military and related, and passenger arrival records—but there are also records relating to land, passports, Indians, claims against the government, and others that can be genealogically useful.

State Records of Birth and Death

Most people are surprised to find out that the making of official records of birth and death is a relatively recent thing, except for New England towns. In New England, such records were begun in most cases with the beginning of the town. But for the most part for the rest of the country, records of birth and death were officially started in the late 1800s and early 1900s, varying from state to state.

The state office handling the centralized state registration of these "vital" records is usually called the State Department of Vital Statistics or the State Board of Health or similar office, usually located in the state capital. Many counties today maintain such records, and large or independent cities may have maintained separate series of birth and death records. But the point to remember is that these records cover a relatively recent period.

Frequently you will already have obtained from home sources the information available from these records. However, it is good practice to secure copies of the available vital records of birth and death even when you think you already know the information they might contain. Home sources and the memories of relatives can be wrong.

Official state records can be in error also, and they frequently are. The author's mother-in-law is recorded in her birth certificate as Elizabeth Rae Stephens, yet her name is Frances, not Elizabeth. Her mother says they talked about using Elizabeth as a name for the baby, but not seriously, and the doctor evidently overheard. Even though they finally settled upon Frances, the name the doctor remembered and reported was Elizabeth. The doctor had been drinking that night, they said, and all the family members enjoy telling how he put down the wrong name. Such stories abound regarding birth certificates. This is not at all intended to discredit totally birth and death records—it is merely a warning. These records provide a wealth of information for the period they cover, but you should be prepared to find inaccuracies from time to time.

Even though birth and death records series did not begin until perhaps 1850 or later, the death records can provide birth information about people born much earlier. For example, a man was born in Mississippi in 1828 at a time when records of birth were not made. He died in 1908 in Texas after vital registration began. His death certificate, if completely filled out, may yield his date and place of birth and the names of his parents as well as dates, places, and facts related to his death and burial. You see how valuable such records can be.

The reliability of the accuracy of the information is as good as the reliability of the person who supplied the information. Usually a next of kin, such as a spouse or child, supplied such information. Often it is disappointing to order a copy of a death certificate and find that in the space on the form for the parents' names, the words "don't know" have been entered.

The government can help you know where to write for certificates of birth, death, marriage, or divorce. Available from the U. S. Government Printing Office, Washington, DC 20402, are the following booklets:

Where to Write for Birth and Death Records   (50¢)

Where to Write for Marriage Records   (50¢)

Where to Write for Divorce Records   (50¢)

These booklets provide the addresses of the offices that can supply copies of records and the cost of both long and short form certificates, if both are available. You are interested in the most detailed of the two certificates. Short forms or birth record cards are primarily intended for the use of living individuals.

County Records

For most of the United States over the years the *county* has been the governmental unit where deeds, wills, and marriages have been recorded. These county records are of great genealogical value.

Marriage Records

In the early years it was often required to have someone post a marriage "bond" before a marriage took place. This legal procedure ensured that there was no legal impediment to the marriage. Marriage "licenses" were also issued before marriage and in some places marriage "intentions" were recorded. Then there is the record of the actual marriage itself, sometimes called the marriage "register" entry or the marriage "return." Thus you will have the opportunity to search for several types of marriage documents.

In these you will find the names of the bride and groom,

which includes the maiden name of the bride. Sometimes the parents' names are stated. Often the father or other relative is a bondsman or a witness. If either the bride or groom were under age, the consent of the parent would be noted. You will obtain the date of the marriage document or the date of the actual marriage, depending on what kind of document you find.

Marriages were not recorded in the counties in all states, but they were in most, and where these records were kept and not later destroyed, they will normally date from the origin of the county. Official marriage records may long pre-date official birth and death records.

Deeds

The succession of land from owner to owner is reflected in deeds and wills. Deeds are frequently helpful in establishing relationships. Deeds also prove that a man lived in a place at a time or over time. Such information is sometimes necessary to prove identities.

An early deed based on the old "metes and bounds" system which used trees, rivers, creeks, and other landmarks as boundary descriptions might include a statement such as, " . . . thence down the meanderings of said creek to a Red Oak in Whittington's Corner, thence down his Father's line to the Beginning. . . . " A deed may even refer specifically to inheritance of the land from a father, uncle, or grandfather, and name that relative as part of the land description. If there had been no other existing record that proved the parentage of the person involved in the land transaction, then such an entry in a deed is a welcome discovery. A further study of the land ownership patterns when reference is made only to "his Father's line" as in the above example would undoubtedly reveal the father's name.

Deeds appear in the official records according to the dates on which they were recorded. Keep in mind that some deeds were never recorded (courthouses were far away, and fees high) while

others might have been recorded many years afterwards. Sometimes original unrecorded deeds may be found in the archives of
a historical society or elsewhere. These are just as valuable to you
as deeds which have been recorded.

The amount of land a man owned, as reflected in the deeds,
gives insight as to his position in the community. Once it is
discovered that a man owned land, it is wise to pursue the land
phase of the problem until it is known how and when he got it,
and what he later did with it. Did he sell it or pass it on through
his will to his children? Of all real property—land—one can
always say: if he had legal title, then he obtained it somehow and
disposed of it somehow. The wise researcher answers these two
questions about all property owned by ancestors: what about the
acquisition, and what about the disposal?

It is also a good idea to try to draw a plat of the land.
Sometimes land plat drawings have survived and are in the
county records. It takes time but is often worth it to plat also the
land of neighbors of the family. This is important particularly
when your ancestor lived in the area during a time period when a
family marriage took place. Most marriages were among neighbors. By knowing who the neighbors were, you will create a list of
surnames to consider as possible related families.

Wills

Wills are wonderful documents for proving relationships. If
only there were more of them! There are many in existence, and
it is a basic part of your search to see if a will exists for your
ancestors. These records, too, are among county records.

There are some tricky things you should know when using
wills. Sometimes a child is not named because his or her share of
property had already been transferred to the son or daughter
during the lifetime of the deceased. Deceased children, particularly those who left no issue, are also usually not named. A
child may have incurred displeasure and have been purposely

left out. Thus the will may not fully reconstitute the family.

The words used in early wills may not have meant the same as they do today. For example, use of the term son-in-law was used to mean stepson as well as the spouse of a daughter. The word nephew was sometimes used to mean grandson or granddaughter as well as nephew in the sense we use it today. Other terms may also have been used differently in the early days. If you find an early document that seems confused, it would be wise to do some reading on early legal terminology. Some of the more advanced genealogical texts treat this in detail.

As with deeds, there are unrecorded wills, and there are also wills which for some reason or other were denied probate. Unrecorded wills may be found anywhere, including among family papers. Wills denied probate will be among the estate papers or recorded in the minutes of the probate court. Look for them and use them.

A will normally has a preamble where the "testator" states what he wants done with his body and debts, then he "devises" land or he "bequeaths" goods and property to his spouse and children and sometimes friends, the "legatees." He names an "executor" or "executrix" (female executor) to administer the estate. Witnesses sign, and most of the time the witnesses were neighbors or relatives or both. A legatee could not be a witness; normally there were at least two witnesses.

Many times not only the will but also related estate papers have survived. These should also be looked at for clues. Ask to see any "loose papers" that may relate to the will or the estate proceeding. After death, an "inventory" of the estate was made, and the property not specifically covered by the will was later sold. The inventory may give the date of death or identify relatives of the deceased person. Lists of the "estate sales" show the names of people who bought items and the amounts they paid. Family members were usually the major purchasers. There may be "accounts" or "distributions" which show that the persons named in the will received what they were entitled to receive.

Persons who died without leaving a will died "intestate." Papers were also created in the disposition of property belonging to such individuals, particularly inventories and sales, property "partitions," and "accounts."

County Court Minutes

The county court minutes often reflect important names, dates, and relationships. The minutes were abbreviated notes taken of the sessions or "court" meetings of the commissioners, sometimes called justices. When the other county records have survived, the minutes may not add much to what has already been learned from the primary documents, such as deeds, wills, and marriage records, yet in the interest of a complete search, the minutes should be looked at. In particular, there may be "depositions" (witness statements) which give an approximate age or a relationship of the person for whom you are looking.

The minutes become of increasingly more value when one or more of the main series of county records have not survived. Minutes are time-consuming to search because they are usually unindexed and must be read page by page. In recent years genealogists have indexed and published some minutes either in full or in abstract form. Before you read a set of minutes, check to see if anyone has prepared an index.

Other County Records

There are other county records, such as orphans court records, tax lists, records of cattle marks and brands, and others. Many times the names used for records and the titles of the offices which created the records are different and/or unique for various parts of the country. You will need to familiarize yourself with such different words as "prothonotary" in Pennsylvania, "chancery clerk" in Mississippi, records of "mesne conveyance" in South Carolina, etc. In Louisiana, counties are termed "parishes." A few minutes of exploration and orientation at a county courthouse will educate you as to the office titles, office jurisdictions, and records terms used in that county.

When you search for county records, remember that county boundaries have changed over time. The same piece of land, owned by the same family, may appear in four or five different counties in the space of thirty years. (State boundaries can shift, too—the same settler's farm will be one year in Mecklenburg County, North Carolina, and the next year in York County, South Carolina, to give one example.) Be sure to check records of "parent" counties and neighboring counties before you decide that nothing is to be found. County origins and parent counties can be found in the following: Joseph Nathan Kane, *The American Counties* (New York, 1960); E. Kay Kirkham, *The Counties of the United States and Their Genealogical Value* (Salt Lake City, 1965); and Everton Publishers, *The Handy Book for Genealogists*, 6th edition (Logan, Utah).

Church Records

When the British immigrated to this country, they brought with them the "parish" concept and the "parish register" where births, christenings, marriages, deaths, and burials were recorded. A good many of the early Episcopal parish registers have survived, and they provide excellent genealogical data. Because the records they cover relate to the early period of colonization and are of value to so many researchers who have descended from these early Americans, most of the extant registers are available today in published form.

Catholic church records are excellent but they are not generally available, although access can usually be obtained by persistent researchers. The Quakers kept good records and many of these have been heavily studied and published.

In the early years of expansion and frontier settlement of the country, there were insufficient numbers of educated ministers to preside over the numerous churches that were springing up. This led to a growth in frontier Protestant churches, such as Baptist and Methodist, the ministry of which did not require the formal education of the Episcopal clergy. Unfortunately these churches were not record keepers. They did create minutes of meetings, which often show when people moved in and out of an area, but there were no official church recordings of births, deaths, burials, or marriages. Such may have been by chance recorded, but not in any planned or organized way. Because of the independence of the individual congregations, the records they created, if they were preserved, went with the ministers. There was no centralized record-keeping office for records to eventually be transferred. Of course over the years many of these records were destroyed, if not by natural causes, then by persons who did not realize their potential historical value. Some of these early church records have survived, however, and today there are church historical associations which seek out, preserve, and make available such early church records.

Family traditions and other records, even the cemetery in which an ancestor was buried, often provide clues to an ancestor's religious connection. When you can determine to which church an ancestor belonged, find out if church records exist for the areas where he lived. When you do not know his religion, it is a good practice to explore among any church records collections available for the area of your research problem.

Naturalization Records

During the colonial period you can sometimes find oaths of allegiance. More detailed records of naturalization are generally available for the 19th and 20th centuries. Though available, they are for the most part difficult to locate. Naturalization could have taken place in any of some 5,000 United States district courts or state or local courts.

Naturalization records can reveal the exact date and place of birth of the person naturalized and sometimes names and ages of family members. Often the name of the ship and date of arrival are given. In other words, such records are usually worth the often tedious effort to obtain a copy.

The National Archives has copies of naturalization proceedings for the states of Connecticut, Maine, Massachusetts, New Hampshire, and Rhode Island, thanks to Work Projects Administration efforts in the 1930s to centralize these records. Some naturalization records have been transferred from U.S. district and circuit courts to the regional archives branches of the National Archives. If you find by consulting the *Guide to Genealogical Records in the National Archives* (1979 edition), that the naturalization records you seek are not in federal archival custody, your next step is to check with the courts themselves where the naturalization may have taken place.

Suggestions for Getting Into Research

1. Write to the National Archives and ask for a) a set of its free leaflets relating to genealogical research; b) sample copies of GSA Form 6751, Order and Billing for Copies of Veteran's Records, and GSA Form 7111, Order and Billing for Copies of Passenger Lists; and c) a free copy of the microfilm catalog *Federal Population Censuses 1790-1890.*

2. Order from the National Archives a copy of the military and related records that may be on file for one of your ancestors (use GSA Form 6751).

3. Search at your local library, at a Mormon branch genealogical library, at a state archives, or at a National Archives regional or D.C. facility, at least one federal census record for one of your ancestral families. Make good notes and look for other related families who may have been living nearby.

4. Order from the appropriate state agency in the state capital, a copy of a birth or death certificate for one of your ancestors.

5. If near to you, visit a county courthouse which served your ancestors and do research among the records there. Or, find out if the records for the county in which you are interested have been microfilmed and are thus available to you at the state archives or are available to you through interlibrary loan at a Mormon branch genealogical library.

12
Genealogical Libraries

There are some very special libraries where genealogists can have a heyday. If you live near one of the large genealogical libraries, you are fortunate indeed. Here you will have access to published genealogies, county histories, general histories, and published abstracts and indexes of various series of records, as well as many other varied research tools.

The New England Historic Genealogical Society, Boston, founded in 1845, currently maintains the largest genealogical book library in the world—a collection of more than 200,000 books and manuscript items. Although specializing in New England families and local history, the library has extensive collections for almost every state and many foreign countries.

Following is a list of a dozen large genealogical collections. There are many other excellent collections in the country. A number of the state libraries usually located in capital cities have very good genealogical collections, and these collections often cover publications relating to other states and foreign countries.

Large historical societies abound in genealogical works. Where state libraries are not strong in genealogical materials, either the state archives, state historical society, or state university library is usually the place where such books are collected for that state. Or, certain specialized libraries exist, such as the Clayton Library in Houston, Texas, which has a tremendously valuable genealogical collection. A minimal amount of investigation will yield the names and locations of good genealogical libraries near you.

New England Historic
  Genealogical Society
101 Newbury Street
Boston, MA 02116

New York Public Library
5th Avenue & 42nd Street
New York, NY 10016

Library of Congress
Washington, DC 20540

Library, National Society,
  Daughters of the
  American Revolution
1776 "D" Street NW
Washington, DC 20006

National Genealogical Society
  Library
1921 Sunderland Place NW
Washington, DC 20036

Western Reserve Historical
  Society
10825 East Blvd.
Cleveland, OH 44106

Public Library of Fort Wayne
  & Allen County
301 West Wayne Street
Ft. Wayne, IN 46802

Newberry Library
60 West Walton Street
Chicago, IL 60610

Burton Collection
Detroit Public Library
5201 Woodward Avenue
Detroit, MI 48202

The Genealogical Society
  Library
50 East North Temple Street
Salt Lake City, UT 84150

Sutro Library
2130 Fulton St.
San Francisco, CA 94117

Los Angeles Public Library
Los Angeles, CA 90017

The Genealogical Society of Utah

The Genealogical Society of The Church of Jesus Christ of Latter-day Saints is known worldwide as the mecca for genealogists. Although the Genealogical Society Library does not hold the world's largest single collection of genealogical books, its microfilm collection coupled with its large book collection makes it the largest genealogical depository in the world.

The Church of Jesus Christ of Latter-day Saints, commonly known as the Mormon or LDS Church, teaches family solidarity and strong family relationships. The Church encourages the organization of family records and their preservation, the writing of personal history, and the record-keeping of personal religious experiences. Members are also given instruction in tracing their ancestry. To assist members in researching their ancestry, the Church started its Genealogical Society in 1894. In the late 1930s, the records microfilming program began.

The Genealogical Society is today engaged in one of the most active and comprehensive genealogical programs ever known to the world. Microfilming is the heart of this extensive genealogical operation. Microfilm photographers are filming records daily in locations the world over. Such documents as land grants, deeds, probate records, marriage records, cemetery records, parish registers, and other records known to be of genealogical value are being filmed. Roughly a million rolls of microfilm have been accumulated thus far, and several thousand new rolls are processed each month. The collection of microfilmed records represents the equivalent of over 4 million printed volumes of 300 pages each!

Through a network of over 300 branch genealogical libraries in the United States and other countries, individuals in pursuit of genealogy in areas served by the branches have access to the main library's microfilm collection. This is accomplished through a well-organized interlibrary loan operation. The branches are located at LDS meetinghouses and are staffed and financially supported by local members of The Church of Jesus Christ of Latter-day Saints. Each branch builds its own collection of available reference books and periodicals. These facilities are graciously made available to all persons.

The significance of these branch genealogical libraries cannot be overstressed. Through them you have access to most of the county records of the United States up to roughly 1850-1900. Later records are normally not filmed in respect of the rights of privacy of living and recently deceased individuals. The federal census records are also available, and to the extent that federal military service and related records have been microfilmed, these are available through the LDS branch genealogical libraries. Do not put off a visit to one of these branch libraries. Find the branch nearest you, and become familiar with the holdings and the film loan procedure.

If you live in a large metropolitan area, chances are there are one or more branch libraries in your area. Look in the telephone directory under Church of Jesus Christ of Latter-day Saints. If you find there is no branch library in your city, write to: Branch Genealogical Libraries, The Genealogical Society, 50 East North Temple St., Salt Lake City, UT 84150. Ask for the name and address of the branch library nearest your area of residence, the name and address of the librarian, the telephone number, and the library hours.

Research in Libraries

Research in libraries can be thrilling, especially when you are lucky enough to find a card catalog entry on the very family or the precise person for whom you are searching. Thousands of genealogies of various shapes and sizes and degrees of accuracy have been published. One or some, perhaps many, of your ancestors have been included. Just because you have never seen or heard of a book on your family, don't use this as an excuse for believing there isn't one. Look first. There just may be one!

The writer once talked the fellow at the next desk at work into getting started on his genealogy. During the same time period, the "genealogy talk" caught the interest of a next door neighbor. What a shock when, after a trip to the library, the neighbor, the man at work, and the author's wife all turned out to be descended from the same man—and the lines of descent for all three were very well set forth in an early published genealogy. I told them all (in jest) that I despised people who could shake their tree and then hold out bushel baskets for the ancestors conveniently to fall into. For most, it always takes hard work to find them. But, you never know when you might find a beautiful book, loaded with relatives. It is a must always to see if you can.

If you do not find a published genealogy, you use another approach. Instead of the *surname* research approach, you use a *locality* approach. Look for published works about the town, county, or state in which your ancestors lived. Many individuals and organizations publish local histories, or they have made and published studies of particular types of records in a locality. You may find that someone has published abstracts of the wills, deeds, or marriage records of the county where your ancestors lived.

There is an important caveat—a strong warning—that all experienced researchers in any field of study are quick to point out. Just because it's published doesn't mean it's right. There are very few perfect books. And because of the enormous amount of detail in a genealogical project, the chances for error are of course greatly multiplied. Genealogies are chock full of facts—hundreds of names, dates, places, relationships, and stories. Multitudinous detail is the heart, the very nature of the effort. Always be aware of the possibility of error in published material, and be eager to check the accuracy of essential data by consulting original records. Remember always that the value of a published genealogical work is related directly to the ease with which you can trace any fact mentioned in it to the original record source.

Generally you may expect from library staffs friendly but

brief orientation and assistance in using catalogs and in finding items. The librarians, however, are not there to do your research for you. Most libraries are understaffed and overworked, and even if they had time, it would not be a wise policy to do research for people. Refrain from the temptation to "unload your problems" onto their shoulders, and be careful not to misconstrue their politeness as interest in your ancestry.

Suggestions for Your Trips to the Libraries

1. Find out from someone you know or from a public librarian what the location is of the nearest large genealogical library. Plan and make a trip to that library.

2. Find out the location of the nearest Mormon branch genealogical library. Visit that branch library and order at least one roll of microfilm on interlibrary loan.

3. Visit your nearest public library and review how libraries work. If there is no genealogical collection, read or review any general histories available.

4. Most all libraries will have at least one or several books on how to do genealogy. Become familiar with them, and make definite plans to read each one through like you would a novel, as time permits.

5. Inquire at a nearby library about, and become familiar with, the reference work by Marion J. Kaminkow, *Genealogies in the Library of Congress, A Bibliography* (Baltimore: Magna Carta Book Co., 1972).

6. Find out at a nearby library what "Nuckmuck" (NUCMC) is and explore the possibility of it being useful to you. NUCMC stands for National Union Catalog of Manuscript Collections.

13

Bridging
The Atlantic

To discover the ancestral home of your immigrant ancestor is one of the major goals of American genealogical research, but often one of the most difficult to achieve. The further back in time the immigration took place, the more complex the problem may become.

Recent immigrants may have left letters and other "home sources" which provide the place of origin. Naturalization records may indicate the home village; passenger arrival lists after 1906 give the passenger's last address in the country from which he came. The 19th century state and county histories with their portraits and biographies (called "mug books" in genealogical circles) will often mention the date and place of birth of a pioneer.

Both for recent and earlier immigrants, it is important to search out in this country references in deeds, wills, or marriage records to a place of birth, or to the names of relatives who stayed behind. Also, in times past families often moved together from one locality to another. Sometimes the place name in the New World reflects the place of origin in Europe, or the hometown of a leading settler or the minister of the group will give a clue to the home parish or county of the humbler folk whom we will find make up the great majority of our ancestors, whether they arrived on the Mayflower or on a passenger vessel during this century.

When you have the fortunate existence of a record naming the exact place in Europe from which the immigrant came, the search in Europe is little different from following migration trails in the United States. You simply pull up stakes and start doing research among the records that exist in that place for the time period in which your ancestor was a resident. If the language is a barrier, you will have to resort to hiring someone to search the records or learn the language.

Family traditions as to old country origins may be misleading. For example, the often repeated story may have included Dublin or Berlin or London as the place of origin. Actually the home place may have been a small village near one of these familiar cities. Even today people still do this. Ask them where they are from and they will say "near Chicago." Or, Liverpool, Bristol, or Hamburg may be given as the place of origin when this is simply the port from which the ship sailed.

In the absence of a known exact place of origin within a country, you will have to "explore." The exploring is done among existing published or unpublished indexes and other finding aids in an attempt to pinpoint one or several localities within the country where the surname was heavily concentrated. By a process of elimination, and hoping for a little luck, the search is thus narrowed down from the whole country to a few smaller jurisdictions.

With common names, the exploring method is normally impractical. It is also impractical for names formed under the various patronymic naming systems. In Denmark an exploring search for Hansens would be futile. The name Hansen was

102

formed from the father's name. Hansen would have resulted from all the fathers named Hans to whom a child was born in a given year, and from men who were not related to each other, although of course some might have been. In early Wales, the name John Richards resulted from the father being named Richard; James Jenkins from a father named Jenkin; Jenkin James from a father named James. Thus all the Richards, the Jenkins, and the Jameses in Wales are not related.

Once a specific locality in which to search has been established, the research can proceed in much the same manner as in this country. There are published genealogies, original records which were created by various levels of governments, and records created by churches and other organizations. There are foreign libraries, archives, historical societies, and genealogical societies, even family organizations. Researchers can be hired, you can visit the libraries and records depositories in person, and a great deal can be accomplished by mail. Don't forget the Mormon branch genealogical libraries. Thousands of rolls of foreign microfilm are available to you in this country through interlibrary loan from the central library facility in Salt Lake City.

If you are fortunate you may be able to trace back some lines several hundred years to perhaps the 16th century. To give you a quick review of history—up to about the 11th and 12th centuries or so, most people used only one name, and records were kept for the most part in relation to only the powerful, the rulers, the churchmen, or the wealthy landowners. Through the years toward the 15th century, the practice of two names came into general use. And gradually more records, particularly legal records, were kept about more people.

In the 16th century the churches in much of Europe began to record events of the common people as well as the rich and powerful. In England, parish registers began to be kept in 1538 (which does not mean that many registers will be found that far back). In some parts of Spain such registers survive from prior to 1500.

If you are able to find the village and pinpoint the church to which your ancestors belonged, you may be able to trace the family back to the beginning of the records. Many people are surprised to learn this is still possible to do in Germany. Everyone remembers the battle scenes from World War II and imagines that all the records went up in smoke. But the planes tried not to strike churches. The bombs were destined for industrial centers in large cities. The tiny churches in the rural villages were largely unmolested. And when they had prior notice, the citizens often carried the church records to safer places. Many of these village church records have survived. Your ancestors more than likely lived in such rural areas before they immigrated.

Recommended Reading

1. Check out of your local library and review or read a good general book on world history, such as William H. McNeill, *A World History* (New York, 1967).

2. Find and scan or become familiar with or read a book about genealogical research in a country from which you know or have reason to believe your ancestors came.

14
Black Genealogy

From the present back to the close of the Civil War in 1865, genealogical research for Blacks follows the same paths as for Whites. Black researchers first exhaust home sources and interview living relatives. They visit cemeteries. They use the same county, state, and federal sources.

The first listing of all Blacks by name in a federal census occurred in 1870, the first census taken following emancipation. In 1850 and 1860, census slave schedules were made, but the schedules did not list the slaves by name. They were tallied by age and sex. These slave schedules are useful, however, in circumstantially proving that a slave of a certain age and sex was the property of a particular owner in a census year.

Free Black heads of household have always been enumerated, beginning with the first census in 1790, and listed by name. Slaves, however, were listed by number in total figures only. That is, you can learn that John Jones had 10 slaves in 1790. In succeeding censuses the enumerations of slaves were further refined with age and sex categories. But, with the exception of free Blacks, names were not recorded until 1870, after the slaves were freed.

For Blacks, research going back beyond the 1870 census is generally quite a challenge. The search is easier for some Black families for the same reasons it is easier for some Whites. The research success difference results from the degree to which the family had wealth, property, position, or education. Black *and* White families with one or several of those characteristics were more likely to have been involved in recorded transactions, and the documents relating thereto may have survived. The city directories of large cities (New York City is one example) may be helpful in distinguishing between free Black families and White families having similar surnames.

Interviews with older living relatives are tremendously important to Blacks. Many of the grandparents and great-grandparents of today's Black senior citizens were born in slavery. These living individuals may have information that will take the research back to a particular county and state, and possibly can pinpoint the name of the last slaveowner prior to emancipation.

Once the slaveowner has been determined, research can be undertaken in the records relating to the owner. Research in the deeds, bills of sale, and the will and probate records of the owner may reveal important information relating to the slave. The migration patterns of White families often reflect the migrations of the slaves.

The search for Black genealogy inevitably consists of a study of White genealogy, which indicates the real need for persons who undertake Black genealogy to become skilled at general genealogical research methods and familiar with general genealogical sources.

The genealogical records of the White owner family must be studied in depth. Any diaries, family bibles, letters, and other papers of the owner families should be thoroughly searched.

These items frequently contain entries relating to the slaves the family possessed.

One early 19th century diary of a South Carolina plantation owner contains detailed entries relating to his slaves. He tells of their illnesses, with what medicines they were treated, and how they progressed. He recorded births, deaths, and marriages of slaves, and frequently mentioned their relationships one to another. He even wrote that he learned about some of his own genealogy from an old house slave who had been with the family for years and had known his great-grandfather. This slave told him where various of his relatives were buried. A White genealogist told the author that he was able to obtain valuable clues about the early generations of his family from an older Black resident of a nearby community who had long been acquainted with his family. He also added that living Whites can often provide much information about Black families.

For Blacks, use of the principle of getting in touch with others who are doing research on the family is not practical at this early point in the development of Black genealogical research. However, Blacks can use this principle explained in an earlier chapter to get in touch with persons who are doing research on the White families with which Blacks were connected.

In some depositories there are records of manumission, that is, documents granting freedom. The Pennsylvania Historical Society has records of thousands of manumissions that were granted before the Civil War. The writer found in the South Carolina archives a torn 1747 manumission whereby Joseph Hasfort recognized 10 years of service and accepted 100 pounds from his mulatto man Abraham and granted him freedom "from the yoke of slavery for ever." The church records kept in German of the Orangeburg, S.C., Church of the Redeemer record the marriage of Abraham Hasfort. There is in S.C. records a manumission record for Elizabeth Hasfort who was a "half-breed Indian woman," and her marriage is also recorded in the records of the Orangeburg Church.

107

Church records can be a significant source for Black genealogy. There were many Black members of White churches, and for a number of years after the war, they attended White churches and are buried in assigned spaces in the church cemeteries. Where church records have survived, they can be useful to Blacks as well as Whites. First, there is a quest to find out what church the family attended, followed by the search to see if any records exist for the church or if any gravestones remain in the cemetery.

At the National Archives in Washington, the records of the Bureau of Refugees, Freedmen, and Abandoned Lands include some valuable items—marriage certificates of recently freed slaves and registers and other records containing information about slave families. The Bureau helped former slaves make the transition from chattel to citizen. The period of the Bureau's greatest activity extended from June 1865 to December 1868. These activities included aiding in regularizing slave marriages, assisting with labor contracts, issuing rations and clothing to destitute freedmen and refugees, leasing land, operating hospitals and freedmen's camps, and providing transportation to refugees and freedmen returning to their homes or relocating them in other parts of the country. As the Bureau developed, it became involved in helping Black soldiers and sailors file and collect claims for bounties, pay arrears, and pensions. These records pertain to such a short period following the Civil War they cannot be considered a major source. They can be helpful, however, to many Black researchers whose ancestors had dealings with the Freedmen's Bureau after the war.

The National Archives has produced two special lists relating to free Blacks. They are Special List 34, *List of Free Black Heads of Families in the First Census of the United States 1790* (Washington, 1973), and Special List 36, *List of Black Servicemen Compiled From the War Department Collection of Revolutionary War Records* (Washington, 1974). These lists relate to less than a thousand Black servicemen in the Revolutionary War, but in 1790 there were roughly some 4,000 free Blacks listed as heads of families. These two special lists are available free from the National Archives.

In recent years the interest in Black history has led to the development of important collections of Black history materials, and these items include names, dates, places, and relationships regarding Blacks. Thus these collections should be investigated by Black researchers.

The search for Black genealogy will amount to an attempt to find the places where the families lived and the names of owners if they were slaves. This will be followed by research among the historical records that have survived for those places. The search itself is little different from the search for White ancestry, but the principal records used as a base will be different and they will be scant.

Read Alex Haley's *Roots,* and when it becomes available read his next book *Search for Roots* which is to give an account of his research path in tracing his ancestry back to Africa. Recently organized is the Afro-American Historical and Genealogical Society, P.O. Box 13006, T Street Station, Washington, D.C. 20009.

part three
Methodology-How To Do It Efficiently And Effectively

15

General History
As An Aid

A knowledge of history greatly helps the genealogical researcher in his quest. The lives of past individuals collectively are the "stuff" of history. Our forebears were parts of social movements and social evolutions, in fact they inevitably were part of everything that ever happened up to now. This is still happening today. We are today a part of tomorrow's history. Our ancestors, as parts of history, make history important in setting the stage for research into the histories of individual families.

Suppose you are a Minnesotan descended from 19th century Swedish immigrants. It will help you to know the story of Scandinavian, particularly Swedish, immigration to this country. When, why, and how did they come?

Your name is Shumate and you are from Southern California. A knowledge of French Huguenot migrations—the whens, whys, wheres, and hows—will help you trace from France over 200 years and across the U.S.A., as you see the de la Chaumette family merge into American society as "Shumates."

They have said you are Scots-Irish. You are a Buchanan. You will want to read the books published about the Scots who crossed the Irish Sea to Ulster, and ultimately migrated to America, pouring "Scots-Irish" blood into the veins of future millions of Americans who would proudly talk of their Scots-Irish ancestry.

You are descended from Jews who migrated eastward out of Germanic-Slavic countries into Russia. Later generations found their way to the Atlantic seaboard of this country. Find out all you can about what has been written about them, what studies have been made, which other Jewish families involved in the same treks have done research and possibly published their own genealogies.

Which roads or trails were in existence at a given time period? Did they possibly go by river or canal? Was land available or workable in an area at a time? When was the county formed? What were the settlement patterns? Did the state grant land to immigrants? Reading and absorbing history will answer these questions and multitudes of others. Maps, especially relief maps, may be of special assistance here also. The answers to the above questions will help you know when, how, and where to look for records that may yield data to help you build a worthwhile genealogy.

In a search for the specific, frequently the search comes to a full stop. You may reach a point where you feel you have exhausted all the sources. At this stage, it can be helpful to move away from "micro" focus and telescope yourself in a reverse direction to take a "macro" view. Upon hearing this point stressed in a lecture, the author tested the theory on a locked-in case.

I began to scan and review materials on the Revolutionary War, particularly as to events surrounding the war in South Carolina. This led to a logical explanation of what had been before a set of troublesome and unexplainable findings. Why, I had wondered, did Lewis Linder leave Orangeburg County, S.C., and go to Dobbs Co., N.C.? Or, did he leave at all? Were there instead two men of the name and time? In studying the history of the Revolutionary War, it was learned that the British moved into Orangeburg in 1780 and established a fort. Many of the area families who had been supporting and fighting for the Colonies left, some going to North Carolina, often to where relatives lived. Some later returned to Orangeburg. This provided a possible explanation for finding a few records over a short time period relating to what appeared to be a South Carolina family in North Carolina records.

The principle involved is known as working from the *general to the specific.* Get a grasp of the general history of the area or of the particular group migration, and work toward finding the name of a specific individual mentioned in a record, such as a land grant. When stumped, move outward and fill in more information on the general history of the time and place. This may provide a clue as to the movement pattern of the general citizenry and lead you to another locality further east or north to look. Remember, you are working from the known to the unknown, thus you are pursuing migrations *backward toward the point of origin.* (When you study general history, you will study it from points of *origin toward destinations.*) See how the study of general history will illuminate your research path?

Assignment

1.   Select a county where an ancestor lived and find and read at least two historical accounts relating to that county.

2.   Read a general history relating to a war in which one of your ancestors was involved.

3.   If your local library does not have a copy, order the following for your files: *The Development of Early Emigrant Trails East of the Mississippi River*, Special Publication No. 3, (12 pp. with map) National Genealogical Society, 1921 Sunderland Place NW., Washington, DC 20036, $2.50.

16
A Note On Heraldry

Nowadays we think of a coat of arms as something to hang on a wall or adorn our jewelry, notepaper, or other personal articles, and they are advertised and sold indiscriminately in this country and elsewhere. Originally, however, when a fighter went into battle or to a tournament, he needed something with which to identify himself, and a distinctive painted shield or cloth coat worn over his armor was used. Thus, from the 11th century there developed a system of heraldry in each of the European countries.

In order to make use of heraldry in our pursuit of genealogy, it is absolutely essential to learn the rules of the particular country or nation where we are working, because these were by no means the same. Originally, individuals simply adopted or "assumed" any arms they liked. After about 1400 the kings and rulers began to grant arms both to individuals and to such entities as towns or universities. In some countries, and particularly Great Britain, assumed arms became to be considered invalid and the only way to obtain a recognized grant of arms was to pay the officers of the king, his heralds, for them. Arms did not always signify nobility by any means, though in general they were sought after and used, especially after the decline of battles and tournaments in armor, as symbols of social prestige.

Heraldry grew to have a language (derived from old French), called "blazon," and a literature all its own. For an introduction to the subject beyond that given by the standard encyclopedias, written in non-technical language, you may wish to look at Dr. Jean Stephenson's *Heraldry for Americans*, published by the National Genealogical Society (Pub. No. 25), or Karl Alexander von Volborth's *Heraldry of the World* (Macmillan, 1974). The latter is very good on the varying systems of heraldry found in different countries.

The right to bear arms was inherited like landed property from father to son and through female heiresses. Because each branch of a family was supposed to make small but distinctive changes in the basic pattern, it is possible to identify the owner of an object, or perhaps trace his parentage from the American colonies to England or elsewhere, by means of a heraldic design. After 1500 these designs could display on one shield the elements of many ancestral lines.

Arms useful to genealogists have been found on seals, tomb monuments and gravestones, tapestries, paintings, clothing, furniture, china and silver, as well as in the reference books of the heralds. Today, however, many persons have made use of arms to which they are not entitled, generally for purely decorative purposes. So long as the law does not protect a property right in arms—an unlikely development in this country and now not common anywhere—such use may be expected to continue. It will be your business to distinguish the proper use of heraldic designs at a time when they were taken seriously, from the modern practices of casual display.

Identity of surname does not carry with it the right legally to use arms. There must also be a proper showing of descent from the person who had the right to bear them. If you are seriously interested in establishing arms of your own, it can be done in various ways. The College of Arms in London and the Cronistas de Armas in Madrid will make grants of new arms to individuals who apply and are prepared to pay the necessary fees.

To those willing to use their eyes, heraldry and its study will not only assist our genealogical and historical studies, but will enhance our appreciation of fine art. We should not be afraid of technical language or social snobbery as we make use of heraldic knowledge for these purposes.

17
The Genealogist's Tools

To help keep track of the information you are finding, you should become familiar with the various forms that genealogists have developed over the years to assist them. The two most used form "tools" are the ancestry (or "pedigree") chart and the family group record. Samples are given on the following pages.

Numerous form styles have come into existence, which makes it necessary for you to look at or use some of them and to ultimately select those forms that best fit your record-keeping needs and tastes. Filling out forms is not your sole aim. Genealogical forms are an aid in keeping records. They will enable you to organize your material and eventually prepare some form of family publication, be it a short typescript paper or report in a folder or a bound printed book.

To learn about the availability of forms for purchase in your area, ask someone you know who is doing genealogy or ask at your local library, historical or genealogical society, or state

ANCESTRY CHART

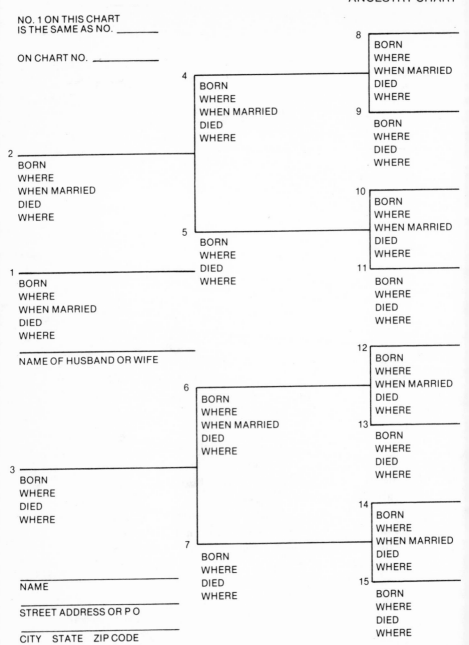

NO. 1 ON THIS CHART
IS THE SAME AS NO. _____

ON CHART NO. _____

8
BORN
WHERE
WHEN MARRIED
DIED
WHERE

4
BORN
WHERE
WHEN MARRIED
DIED
WHERE

9
BORN
WHERE
DIED
WHERE

2 _____
BORN
WHERE
WHEN MARRIED
DIED
WHERE

10
BORN
WHERE
WHEN MARRIED
DIED
WHERE

5
BORN
WHERE
DIED
WHERE

11
BORN
WHERE
DIED
WHERE

1 _____
BORN
WHERE
WHEN MARRIED
DIED
WHERE

_____
NAME OF HUSBAND OR WIFE

12
BORN
WHERE
WHEN MARRIED
DIED
WHERE

6
BORN
WHERE
WHEN MARRIED
DIED
WHERE

13
BORN
WHERE
DIED
WHERE

3 _____
BORN
WHERE
DIED
WHERE

14
BORN
WHERE
WHEN MARRIED
DIED
WHERE

7
BORN
WHERE
DIED
WHERE

15
BORN
WHERE
DIED
WHERE

_____
NAME

_____
STREET ADDRESS OR P O

_____
CITY   STATE   ZIP CODE

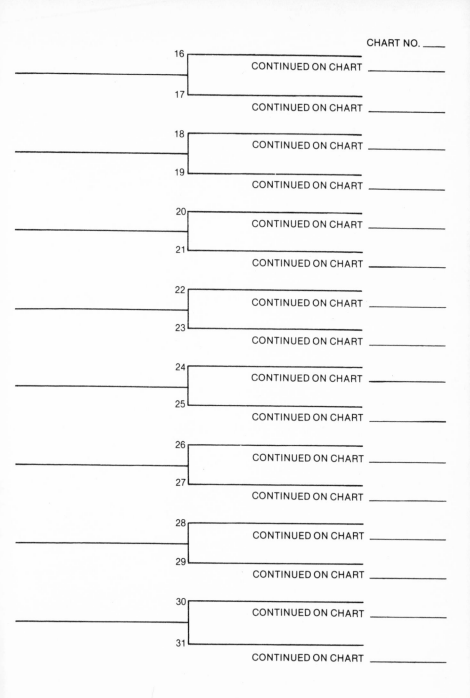

CHART NO. _____

16

CONTINUED ON CHART _____

17

CONTINUED ON CHART _____

18

CONTINUED ON CHART _____

19

CONTINUED ON CHART _____

20

CONTINUED ON CHART _____

21

CONTINUED ON CHART _____

22

CONTINUED ON CHART _____

23

CONTINUED ON CHART _____

24

CONTINUED ON CHART _____

25

CONTINUED ON CHART _____

26

CONTINUED ON CHART _____

27

CONTINUED ON CHART _____

28

CONTINUED ON CHART _____

29

CONTINUED ON CHART _____

30

CONTINUED ON CHART _____

31

CONTINUED ON CHART _____

archives. If you do not find forms available locally, write for a supplies catalog from Everton Publishers, P.O. Box 368, Logan, UT 84321; or Goodspeed's Book Shop, Inc., 18 Beacon St., Boston, MA 02108.

The Ancestry Chart

The ancestry chart provides a skeletal outline of your direct ancestral lineage. The most popular form begins with you on the left side of the form and flows to the right, dividing first into space for recording vital data (birth, marriage, and death) on your parents, then grandparents, etc. Record the male (paternal) names on top of each pair of lines; the females (maternal) in the lower spaces.

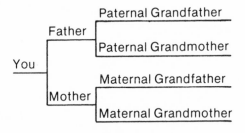

The ancestry or pedigree chart—it is widely called "pedigree" but this author prefers "ancestry"—is an extremely useful and handy way to keep track of where you are and where you are headed in your quest. It is wise to keep your ancestry charts up-to-date, adding new information as you find it.

The ancestry chart contains data on direct line ancestral couples only. Information on whole families is recorded on the family group record form.

Family Group Record

The family group record form is used to record data on whole single family units. Space is provided to record vital data on the husband, wife, and each child in the family. The practice is to complete a family group record form for each ancestral couple on the ancestry chart.

There are standards used by most genealogists for recording information on the forms. Record names in full. Record maiden names of females. Record dates in the order of day, month, year, not using numbers for months: 28 Jan 1837. Record places in the order of town, county, and state: Kenedy, Karnes Co., Tex.

It is also important to learn early and to firmly establish the habit of recording on the form the sources of the data entered on the family group record.

Recording Information on Family Group Record Forms

The family group record form illustrated in this chapter is the one preferred by the author. The reason may be that a form very similar to this one was the first such form introduced to me, and I am used to working with it. You will have a selection of forms available to you to choose from. Following are instructions for recording data on the form illustrated. Even though the form you select to use may be different in format, most of the ideas given for recording information will still be useful.

Recording Names on the Family Group Record Form

SURNAME

Some people like to record the surname in capital letters, followed by a comma, then the given name(s). *Do not abbreviate any part of the name.*

HUSBAND _____

Born _____ Place _____
Marr. _____ Place _____
Died _____ Place _____
Bur. _____ Place _____

HUSBAND'S
FATHER _____
HUSBAND'S
MOTHER _____
HUSBAND'S
OTHER WIVES _____

WIFE _____

Born _____ Place _____
Died _____ Place _____
Bur. _____ Place _____
WIFE'S
FATHER _____
WIFE'S
MOTHER _____
WIFE'S
OTHER HUSB.

SEX M F	CHILDREN List Each Child (Whether Living or Dead) in Order of Birth	WHEN BORN DAY MONTH YEAR	WHERE BORN TOWN
1			
2			
3			
4			
5			
6			
7			
8			
9			
10			
11			
12			

SOURCES OF INFORMATION

NAME & ADDRESS OF PERSON SUBMITTING RECORD

NECESSARY EXPLANATIONS

	COUNTY	STATE OR COUNTRY	DATE OF FIRST MARRIAGE TO WHOM		WHEN DIED		
				DAY	MONTH		YEAR

OTHER MARRIAGES

Example.   DOE, John Hamilton

Others prefer to write the name down as it sounds when spoken, either capitalizing or not capitalizing the surname.

Example.   John Hamilton DOE

INITIALS

Do not record initials if the given name for which an initial stands can be found. In instances where an initial is actually known to be a given name in itself, place the initial(s) in quotation marks and do not use the period mark.

Example.   JONES, "B J"

SEVERAL GIVEN NAMES

The space for recording names of Husband and Wife is sufficient for long names; and the space for recording names of Children is wide enough for a double line of entry when necessary. Use a diagonal following the last given name on the lower line and in front of the next given name in the space above to indicate the continuity of given names.

SEX M F	CHILDREN List Each Child (Wheather Living or Dead) in Order of Birth
1 M	/Garlington Tatum EVANS, Mark William Thomas/

NICKNAMES

When, in order to adequately identify an individual, it is necessary to record his nickname, note it in the space provided for "Necessary Explanations" as illustrated.

128

```
┌─────────────────────────────────────────────┐
│ ┌───────────────────────────────────────────┐ │
│ │ NECESSARY EXPLANATIONS                      │ │
│ │ #1 Christopher also known by "Kit"          │ │
│ └───────────────────────────────────────────┘ │
└─────────────────────────────────────────────┘
```

SHORT FORMS OF GIVEN NAMES

Do not record diminutive forms of given names, e.g., Jack for John, Bill for William, Betty, Betsey, or Beth for Elizabeth, etc., unless it is known that the diminutive form is actually the given name. When it is, underline the given name to indicate that it has been recorded correctly.

Example.   FRANCIS, Jack Don

UNCOMMON GIVEN NAMES

Underline uncommon or unusual given names. If a female Child was given a male name or a male Child was given a female name, underline both the sex designation and the given name.

SEX M F	CHILDREN List Each Child (Whether Living or Dead) in Order of Birth
1 F	SUTTON, Tommy Joe
2 M	SUTTON, Bruce
3 M	SUTTON, Shirley
4	

TITLES

Titles are often valuable for adequate identification and may be recorded in parentheses in abbreviated form before the first given name. If military rank is involved, record the highest attained.

> *Examples.*　COFFEY, (Maj) Alan Edward
> FLANAGAN, (Dr) Gerald Smith
> MIDGLEY, (Lt) Stephen
> BUTLER, (Judge) William
> ADAMS, (Rev) Richard

OCCUPATIONS

The principal occupation of the Husband is an important item of identification. Record it in parentheses in the available space following his name.

HUSBAND NEUHAUSER, Horst   (teacher)
Born _____ Place _____
Marr. _____ Place _____
Died _____ Place _____
Bur. _____ Place _____

OTHER MARRIAGES OF HUSBAND AND WIFE

If the Wife was married more than once, enter in parentheses before the name of the Husband the chronological number of his marriage to the Wife to indicate which Husband of the Wife he is, i.e., first husband, second husband, etc.

WIFE (1) PECK, Rachel
Born _____ Place _____

Similarly, if the Husband was married more than once, enter the chronological number of the Wife before her name to indicate if she is the first wife, second wife, etc.

130

HUSBAND (2) GARLINGTON, Conway

Born _____ Place _____

NAMES OF CHILDREN

Enter names of Children consecutively in the order of birth.

DESIGNATION OF SEX

Indicate the sex of each Child in the space provided, using the letter M for a male Child and the letter F for a female Child. If the sex of a Child is unknown, record the Child in the proper chronological order of birth, with a question mark in the space provided for the designation of sex. It is not wise to assume the sex based on the Child's name.

MULTIPLE BIRTHS

If two or more Children were born to a couple on the same day, enter the word *twin, triplet*, etc., in parentheses following the given names.

4			
	M	BRICK, John (twin)	22 Aug
5			
	M	BRICK, Joseph (twin)	22 Aug

STILLBORN CHILDREN

Enter the names of stillborn Children in the normal chronological order of birth, with the word *stillborn* in parentheses following the given name(s).

131

1			
	F	HAILEY, Ruth Ann	
2			
	F	HAILEY, Susan (stillborn)	

NAMES OF SPOUSES OF CHILDREN

Record the full name of the spouse of each Child in the space provided.

	DATE OF FIRST MARRIAGE	WHEN DIED DAY MONTH YEAR
STATE OR COUNTRY	TO WHOM	
	JOHNSON, Martha Jane	

If a Child was married more than once, enter the figure 1 in parentheses before the name of the first spouse of the Child.

	(1) WILSON, Rebecca Anne

NAMES OF OTHER SPOUSES OF CHILDREN

Record the names of other spouses of Children in the space provided at the bottom of the form designated "Other Marriages."

OTHER MARRIAGES
#6 Enoch md (2) 24 Dec 1916 JONES, Jane

CHILDREN WHO DID NOT MARRY

If a Child lived to be of marriageable age and it is definitely known that the Child *did not marry*, enter this information in the space provided for the recording of the name of the spouse.

	DATE OF FIRST MARRIAGE	WHEN DIED DAY MONTH YEAR
STATE OR COUNTRY	TO WHOM	
	did not marry	
	ANDREWS, Elizabeth	
	(1) HINTON, Julius	

Recording Dates on the Family Group Record Form

DAY, MONTH, YEAR

Record dates in the order of *day*, *month*, and *year* with the month abbreviated. Periods are not necessary following the abbreviations. It is recommended that the month of June be spelled out in full to avoid any confusion between "Jun" and "Jan."

Example.   16 Feb 1792

UNDERLINING OF DATES

There will be times when correctly recorded dates will appear to be in conflict with other dates. When this occurs, underline the dates appearing to be in conflict to indicate that they have been recorded correctly.

Example 1.   If a comparison of the date of marriage of the Husband and Wife and the date of birth or christening of the first child indicates that there is an interval of less than nine months between these dates, underline the date of marriage and the date of birth or christening.

Example 2.   If a Child was born after the death of the Husband or was christened after the death of the Husband or Wife, underline the dates concerned.

CALCULATING YEARS OF BIRTH

If the date of birth is unknown, the year of birth may be *calculated* based upon a known age at a dated event in the life of the individual.

Example.   Reuben Taylor was listed as age 32 in the census of 1850. The calculated year of birth of Reuben Taylor would be 1818.

HUSBAND TAYLOR, Reuben

Born _____(32-1850) 1818_____ Place _____
Marr. _____ Place _____
Died _____ Place _____

If age in years at death is known, the calculated year of birth may be recorded. To show the basis for the calculated date, enter the word *age* and the age at death following the date of death.

WIFE _____

Born _____1790_____ Place _____
Died _____12 May 1860 age 70_____ Place _____

If the precise age at death or burial is known, the exact date of birth may be calculated. In the space designated "Necessary Explanations," note the age at death or burial as illustrated:

134

HUSBAND _____

Born _____ 10 June 1875 _____ Place _____
Marr. _____ Place _____
Died _____ 20 July 1922 _____ Place _____

NECESSARY EXPLANATIONS
Husband age 47 years, 1 month,
10 days at death

CALCULATED YEARS OF BIRTH OF CHILDREN

If age at marriage is known, calculate the year of birth. To show the basis for the calculated date, enter the age at marriage and the year of marriage in parentheses above the calculated year of birth as illustrated:

WHEN BORN			DATE OF FIRST MARRIAGE
DAY	MONTH	YEAR	TO WHOM
		(25-1862)	14 July 1862
		1837	

If age at census is known, calculate the year of birth. Enter the age given in the census and the year of the census in parentheses above the calculated year of birth as illustrated:

WHEN BORN		
DAY	MONTH	YEAR
		(38-1860)
		1822

If age in years at death is known, calculate the year of birth. Following the date of death enter the word *age* and the age at death as illustrated:

WHEN BORN			WHEN DIED		
DAY	MONTH	YEAR	DAY	MONTH	YEAR
		1863	17 Mar 1896 age 33		

If the precise age at death is known, calculate the exact date of birth. In the space for "Necessary Explanations," note the age at death.

> *Example.* (Recorded in "Necessary Explanations") #1 William, age 85 years, 3 months, 10 days at death

APPROXIMATING YEARS OF BIRTH

When a year of birth has been *approximated* based on the "preponderance of the evidence" available, the abbreviation *abt* should be entered preceding the approximated year of birth as illustrated:

HUSBAND _____
Born _____ abt 1794 _____ Place _____
Marr. _____ Place _____

MARRIAGE DATES

Known marriage dates should be recorded in the spaces provided as illustrated. It is normally wise not to clutter the space with approximated marriage dates, but is preferable to leave the space open until a date is located.

HUSBAND _____

Born _____	Place _____
Marr. _____17 May 1812_____	Place _____
Died _____	Place _____

	DATE OF FIRST MARRIAGE	WHEN DIED DAY MONTH YEAR
STATE OR COUNTRY	TO WHOM	
	13 Mar 1837	

MARRIAGE BANNS, BONDS, INTENTIONS, LICENSES, ETC.

If the precise date of marriage is unknown and it is definitely known that a couple married, either the date of issuance of the marriage license, the date of making of the marriage bond or allegation, or the date of proclamation of banns, etc., should be recorded in the space provided for recording the date of marriage. Preceding the date of the pre-marriage document, an abbreviated entry should be made indicating the type of document to which the date entered refers. Following are recommended abbreviations which can be used in the recording of pre-marriage documents.

Banns	bns
Bond	bnd
Intentions	int
License	lic
Proclamations	prc

HUSBAND _____

Born _____	Place _____
Marr. _____lic 14 Jan 1815_____	Place _____

REFERENCING OTHER MARRIAGES

All *other marriages* of the Husband and Wife should be referenced in the space designated "Husband's Other Wives" and "Wife's Other Husbands" by entering the chronological number of the marriage followed by the date of the marriage and the name of other husband or wife.

WIFE'S MOTHER
WIFE'S OTHER HUSB (2) 5 July 1863 JOHNSON, William Raymond

All *other marriages* of Children should be referenced in the space designated "Other Marriages" as illustrated:

OTHER MARRIAGES
#5 Samuel md (2) 14 Mar 1796 ASKEW, Jane

DIVORCES

If it is known that a marriage ended in divorce, note this information by entering the abbreviation *div* for "divorced" in parentheses following the date of the marriage.

	DATE OF FIRST MARRIAGE	WHEN DIED DAY MONTH YEAR
STATE OR COUNTRY	TO WHOM	
	10 Sep 1912 div	
	WILSON, Martha Ann	

DATES OF DEATH AND BURIAL
UNKNOWN

In the absence of the definite date of death or burial:

> *If the date of the proving of the individual's will is known,* record that date, with the abbreviation *wp* for "will proved" as illustrated. Record the date the will was made (*wd* for "will dated") in the space for the death date, and the date the will was proved in the space for the burial date. Record the name of the county and state where the will was made, and the book and page number, in the space provided for the place of death.

Died __wd 17 Apr 1756__ Place __Bk 1, Pg 56 Halifax Co., N.C.__
Bur __wp 22 June 1757__ Place _____ ,, _____ ,, _____
HUSBAND'S
FATHER _____

If no information is found regarding a will, the date of an "Inventory of Possessions" or the date of granting of "Letters of Administration" may be recorded, preceded by the abbreviation *inv* for "inventory" or *adm* for "letters of administration."

Recording Places on the Family Group Record Form

TOWN, COUNTY, STATE

Places should be recorded in the order of *town (or parish), county (or foreign equivalent),* and *state (or country).*

_____ Place __Marshfield, Plymouth, Mass._____
_____ Place _____

When entering the names of places of birth of Children, it may be necessary to abbreviate the county and state.

WHERE BORN		
TOWN	COUNTY	STATE OR COUNTRY
Three Rivers	Live Oak	Texas
San Antonio	Bexar	Texas
Manassas	Fairfax	Va
	Fauqu.	Va

Assignment

1. Buy, borrow, or order some ancestry charts and family group record forms. (The forms illustrated here are available from the Correspondence Branch (NNCC), National Archives, Washington, DC 20408. As of this writing, the price was 2 cents per sheet, with a minimum billing of $3, but payment in advance can be made for less than that amount.)

2. Fill out charts and forms on the first three or four generations of your ancestry.

18
The Early Handwriting

There are a few early handwriting practices you will need to learn about as your search gets under way. As you progress back towards the early Colonial period there are more variations, some of which are interesting and unique. Becoming adept at reading and deciphering the early handwriting is one of the more pleasing aspects of your genealogical study. There is a certain ineffable satisfaction derived from being able to read the old handwriting at a glance. Once you have worked with a few old documents, see if you understand the feeling I am trying to convey.

The earliest scribes worked their written communications into clay tablets, and some of these survive today. Your work will be a genuine success if you can proceed back to the point where you will need to learn to decipher information from clay tablets! Several hundred years ago the official language for official documents was almost entirely Latin. As time progressed, the officials of government determined that writing should become more simple in official papers, using less Latin, so that ordinary people could understand. This was part of the social revolution and evolution that brought more and more people into intelligent participation in affairs concerning them. The old Latin influence is still seen today by our modern use of such symbols as the ampersand (&) and the "at" sign (a), found on all type-writers.

There was a general break towards the end of the 16th century—what was written earlier you will normally find extremely difficult to read without long practice, and even the pre-1660 work of scribes trained in earlier schools or styles will be troublesome.

The "schools" mentioned were handwriting schools. Not everyone could write in the early years; in fact during a period of history it was not fashionable for a gentleman to learn to write. Few women were taught to write, even among the nobility. This social attitude was brought to the Colonies. The ideal of literacy in early America was for a man to be able to read the Bible to his family and to know enough arithmetic to be able to deal at the market place in selling his produce. In lieu of writing himself, a man had scribes do his writing for him. People were paid to write—and were hired on their ability to write well, and fast. With only a small percentage of the population able to write, of course the more artistic and faster scribes were in demand. The profession of scribe (scribner) was highly respected. The scribes were paid by the word or by the line, which led to the superfluous use of words in the early documents.

Handwriting as a profession was taught in the schools by writing masters. These masters developed their own styles of handwriting for their schools. There was even competition and rivalry among writing masters. Writing became an art form, with artistic touches, swirls, flourishes, and even shadings. The objective was to create impressive looking documents. The social changes mentioned saw the beauty in documents gradually give way to hurriedly prepared, much abbreviated documents as more people learned to write and as the county clerks and recorders

142

resorted to signs, symbols, and abbreviations to reduce the time spent on documents.

In the early years our ancestors used for pens turkey, duck, and even hen feathers. To sharpen these "quills," they used a "pen knife" which resulted in the word penknife that we use today to refer to a small pocketknife. These quills could not hold enough ink to last a long period of time, thus a clerk had to write as fast as he could. In so doing, he often ran words together. This is a source of our difficulty in deciphering much of the early handwriting.

The scribes and later the court clerks exercised a genuine "freedom" of writing style in their punctuation, which is often nonexistent, and in capitalization. Words will be found capitalized at random, with no apparent consistency or thought to any capitalization rules. You will find proper names, both of people and places, sometimes not capitalized; and you will find common nouns and other words capitalized in the middle of a sentence.

One of the first strangers you will meet will be the long "s" (ſ). This will appear in old documents, even the federal census records that will be among the first records you will consult. You will see what looks to you like "fs," "f," double "f," or "p." Most of the time the long "s" interpreted means double "s" (ss), as in Jesse or Rosser, which written in the document may look like Jefse Rofser.

The long "s," looking very much like today's "f," was also often used to mean one "s," when the "s" was not double, as in Frafer (Fraser). The long "s" usage is often an indexing hazard. For example, in a published index the name Hosfort appeared as Hoffort, which was caused by a handwriting deciphering problem.

The long "s" was seldom used at the beginning of words. A final "s" at the end of a word may be a mere squiggle or up-curve after the letter before. This causes real problems in deciding such things as whether the writer meant Parkes or Parker.

Another stranger you will find early in your search in census records will be the abbreviation for ditto, written either "do" or with the second letter upraised (d°). Some other abbreviations and their meanings are:

J^r , Jun ^{r} , Jun	Junior	Y^e	The
s d	said	Y^t	That
afs ^{d}	aforesaid	W^n	When
admon:	administration	Y^m	Them
admin ^{r}	administrator	W^{ch}	Which
exec ^{r}	executor	Impr ^{s}	Imprimus (in the first place)
inv:	inventory		
p^r	per		

Abbreviations were also used to indicate given names. The following were commonly used name abbreviations. The list is not exhaustive, but it will show you the general pattern of forming abbreviations and will give you an idea of what to watch for.

Abra ^{m}	Abraham	Jas, Ja ^{s}	James
And ^{w}	Andrew	Jno, J^n	John
Benj a , Benj ^{n}	Benjamin	Jos, Jo ^{s}	Joseph
Cath^e	Catherine	Marg ^{t}	Margaret
Cha ^{s}	Charles	Mich ^{l}	Michael
Christ ^{n}	Christian	Rich^d	Richard
X^r , Xtopher, Xopher	Christopher	Sam ^{l}	Samuel
Dan ^{l}	Daniel	Tho ^{s}	Thomas
Erasm ^{s}	Erasmus	W^m , Will ^{m}	William

The colon was used to signify the omission of one or more letters from a word or a part of a given name, such as Dan: (meaning Daniel). A wavy line over a "u" (ũ) was sometimes used to distinguish the u from an m or n. A dot above a word indicated a whole stop. A dot between words indicated there was supposed to be a separation in phrases; in this case we use a comma today. A dot on the line meant a brief pause. A line over the place where there should have been a double letter is often found, particularly in connection with the letters m and n, such as in cañon (cannon) and com̃on (common). To divide a word at the end of a line, rather than a hyphen, you may find an equals sign (=).

Numbers, too, were written differently. Sevens often looked like nines. Eights used to lay over on their sides, toward the right. Sevens and ones and sevens and fours are often confused in the interpretation, also the six could look like today's four because of the way the pen stroke formed the bottom part of the number.

Several capital letters are troublesome. The capitals L and T are often indistinguishable; likewise the capitals I and J, L and S, M and N, T and F, and U and V are often quite confusing. A good idea in such instances is to scan the document and become familiar with the way the writer formed certain letters. Try to match the handwriting in one place with another, or if you think you see a part of a letter but are not sure, look around on the document to see how the writer formed that letter in some word that you can decipher. You must become familiar with the writer's style.

Look for familiar words and phrases in the document— names, places, legal phraseology, dates, and regnal years. Pay particular attention to phrases likely to be repeated in every example of a will, deed, or parish register, and see how the letters are made. For example, the phrase "To All To Whom These Presents Shall Come, Greeting" will be found at the beginning of many documents. Knowing this, you have a bench mark to return to as a source for learning how certain letters were formed by that clerk.

When a document is extremely difficult to decipher, a work-able procedure is to start at the beginning and read straight through, picking up what you can read and understand. Do not try to move too fast. At this point forget the words you cannot make out. Read the document over several times in a general scanning way. Gradually it will begin to make sense to you. As it becomes clearer to you, more words will come into focus, and you will get more and more out of it.

Where you are doing a great deal of work on one source, such as a county deed or will book, become familiar with the handwriting and abbreviations used by each clerk, as they will differ. Where possible and as necessary, refer to the original documents. Even good microfilms may add confusion ("print-through" of writing on back, shadows, faded ink). This added confusion not in the original may make what was already diffi-cult writing impossible to read on the microfilm.

Recommended Reading

E. Kay Kirkham, *How to Read the Handwriting and Records of Early America* (Salt Lake City, 1964).

19
Abstracting Information From Documents

The availability of copying machines will help you obtain many photostatic and electrostatic copies of documents. However, cost, storage, and handling make it impractical to obtain photocopies of all relevant documents. This is why we abstract information from documents to use in our files.

The document is before you. It is long. It has more information than you want or need. But what do you copy from it? The answer to this significant question is given here.

Usually it is a waste of time to copy the entire contents of most documents. In the interest of time, storage space, and manipulation of collected information, you need to take down only pertinent information, but you must be careful to get every piece of important information.

You will at times copy all or part of a document verbatim. When you copy everything, you are making an *extract*. When you extract, you transcribe the entire document, paragraph, or sentence as you see it. At other times you will *abstract*. When you abstract, you pull out of the document specific items of information but you do not copy everything as you see it. When abstracting, non-substantive information and fringe words are dropped.

An *extract*: 'This Indenture made this 23rd day of September in the year of our Lord one thousand Seven hundred and Eighty-one between John Shaw of Anson County in the State of North Carolina of the one part and James Young of the said county and State of the other part ...."

This information could be shortened for our files by *abstracting*: Deed, 23 Sep 1781, John Shaw of Anson Co., N.C., to James Young, same county.

The above examples do not illustrate how to deal with all of the information contained in deeds, but they do show you the principle of *ab*stracts vs. *ex*tracts. Note that the *ex*tracted information is enclosed in quotation marks; the *ab*stracted information is not.

You will frequently use a combination of extracts and abstracts in transcribing information from a single document. Some parts of a document may be significant, impressive, or interesting, and you wish to preserve the entire portion. Remember to enclose this portion in quotation marks.

There is a way to combine the principles of both extracting and abstracting. The *extract/abstract*: "This Indenture ... (23 Sep 1781) ... between John Shaw of Anson County ... (N.C.) ... and James Young ... (same county)...." Note that elisions, words dropped out, are noted by three periods. Information shortened or interpreted is in parentheses. This type of extracting in abstract style preserves the original flow of the information in the document. Some fringe words are kept so that the abstract holds together in more or less sentence fashion. When used in a published work in this format, the extract is easy to read and has a professional and credible look, even though the information value of the facts cited is the same as it would have been for a typical abstract.

From here on in this chapter, the word abstracting will be

used as a generic term to refer to the taking of information from documents, but understand it to include extracting and the combination extract/abstract.

The next chapter on notetaking talks about the following, but it needs to be mentioned here. When abstracting, always note at the top of your notepaper, preferably the right-hand side, the surname that is the subject of the search and the locality involved. On the top line, make a heading which can key you to the place where the research is being done, the date you are making the search, and the type of record. Always record the volume or book number and the page number where the document was found. This may be a folder, folio, or other number, or a microfilm number.

SHAW
Anson Co.,
N.C.

Anson Co. Deeds (N.C. State Archives, Raleigh, 15 Apr 1977)

Book A,   "This Indenture . . . (23 Sep 1781) . . . between
Page 31   John Shaw of Anson County . . . (N.C.) . . . and
            James Young . . . (same county). . . ."
Mic. Roll
No. 15

The objective is to gather out of a document all relevant names, dates, places, relationships and any significant descriptions of the person or family or their possessions, particularly occupations and land descriptions. Consider not only present needs but possible future information needs. For the moment you may be content with finding the specific unit of data you were looking for. But the document may offer more that you should take down. It is far more efficient to get everything useful at one time than to go back to the same document later to obtain remaining information.

Use abbreviations freely in your abstracting, but those that make sense to you and will to others. Use standard or popular abbreviations as much as possible. Use "sic" to denote that's the way it was when something appears out of place, odd, or erroneous. Don't make changes; copy what you see, even when you know the spelling or date is wrong. When signatures are indicated with "X" or other marks, retain this information in your notes. If you are dealing with an original document rather than a court recorded copy in the handwriting of the court clerk, consider the utility of a photostat or electrostatic (Xerox) copy of the signatures. Comparisons of signatures may provide valuable proof of identity of a man who executed documents considerably separated in space or time.

Following are ideas for abstracting information from two types of significant research documents—deeds and wills. This will help you grasp what type of information should be abstracted for your genealogical research files.

Deeds

From deeds, the following information, when given, should be abstracted:

County and state of transaction   Date deed was written

Volume and page number   Date deed was acknowledged

Name of grantee   Date deed was recorded

Grantee's county of residence   Location and description
           of land

Grantee's social status or
occupation ("gentleman,"
"planter," "yeoman,"
"blacksmith")

Name of grantor

Grantor's county of residence

Grantor's social status or
occupation

No. of acres involved

Price

Names of prior land holders
(often part of, or noted
following, the description)

Names of adjoining land
owners

Names of witnesses

Relevant information from the
"dower release," particularly
wife's name

Acknowledgment of
consideration paid

When consulting deed indexes, you will normally find separate "grantee" and "grantor" indexes. Be sure to note at the top of your entries copied from such indexes whether they are grantor or grantee entries.

For deeds it is useful to *ex*tract the land description portion of the deed. This is a specific description and you may need it in its entirety. The following illustrates the manner in which the author made an extract/abstract of a Virginia deed:

Brunswick Co., Va., Deed Bk. No. 4 (Va. State Lib., 18 July 1975)

p. 107   "I Thomas Tatum of Brunswick County Planter for . . . five Pounds . . . paid . . . by William Fox of the same County . . . sell . . . unto . . . William Fox . . . fifty Acres . . . more or lefs . . . in the County of Brunswick and is part of that Tract . . . I now live on . . . Beginning at a Beech on the East Side of the Beech Island Gut at the Mouth of a Sink that makes into the said Gut thence down the said Gut as it meanders to Fountains Creek thence down the said Creek as it meanders to William Weavers Corner on the said Creek thence from the Creek along his line South forty eight Degrees

East Ninety Poles to Avents Corner thence along his line North fifty three Degrees East ninety eight Poles to a red Oak thence North one Degree East to a made Corner of a parcell of Trees choped inwards thence along a line of mark Trees to the Beginning . . . (26 Mar 1750) . . . in Presence of John Peterson John (his I mark) Saul James (his I mark) Duglafs" Court 27 Mar 1750 Ordered to be Recorded.

Wills

In using wills, it is a good idea to look at the original will and all "loose papers" and records that may exist relating to the settlement of the estate. In the various papers you may find much useful information and good leads. From the will itself you will want to abstract:

County and state of document

Volume and page number, also estate or jacket number, if applicable

Testator's name

Date will made

Date will proved

Date will recorded (if different)

Physical condition of testator

Social status or occupation of testator

Residence of testator and legatees

Any land descriptions or plantation names

Every name, in the order given

Every indication of relationship

Every indication of a child or other relative under age

Preserve pronouns, such as *my* son

What was given to each legatee

Name of executor or executrix

Name of guardian or overseer appointed for children

Special situations, such as a
   child or other mentally
   incompetent relative

Names of witnesses
   (customarily three,
   might be two or four)

20
Notetaking
And Filing

You will find yourself making notes on the backs of used envelopes, library call slips, and pieces of paper sacks. But that's o.k. The thought will bring a shudder to any pros who might read this, but they do it, too. Information comes at unpredictable times, and we all do the best we can with whatever "equipment" might be available. One professional admitted that he is quite good at making notes using the inside of his Kool cigarette package!

Using a familiar accounting term, you will later "post" that information from the homespun notes to your files. Your files will be composed of proper genealogical notes. Which brings us to our topic for this chapter. What are proper notetaking and filing procedures?

There seems to be almost universal agreement among genealogical researchers that it is a good practice to use standard business-size paper for notes (8½" x 11"). It is also a widespread practice to write the surname on the top right-hand corner of the page as the first item of business. Next, across the top of the first line, place the source reference. This is a full reference describing the source or the source document. Its purpose is to provide the information needed to find the source or document again when needed—by you or by anyone who will in the future use your notes or your publications.

Typically the source reference will contain first the specific title or name of the record type or "record group," a term used in archival institutions, and will list as many descriptive levels as is practical or necessary to find the record again. For documents, there may be a volume or folder (folio or liber) number, a specific page number, and if on film, a microfilm number. For books, put down following or before the title, the author's name. Include the publisher, the date of publication, and the city of publication. If more than one volume exists, include a volume number, and note if a second or third edition, etc. All of this is important to have for use in citing the information you will relate in any written report, article, or other work you may produce on the family or individual. Some do not bother to do the following but many recommend it and your author agrees—record also the depository where the research is being performed and the date.

It saves time to set up the source reference in the style it may be used when citing references in future written material you may produce. In fact, the best notes are those that have been created while having in mind the future use of the notes. In other words, plan your notetaking fully to serve your needs. Prepare notes so that they will fit right into your filing scheme, and so that they can be used as immediate sources from which genealogical research papers, articles, and books can be produced. (The essential procedures and basic principles for abstracting information from documents to put in your notes has been set forth in a separate chapter.)

It has been stated before but you need to hear it again. Remember to leave the data you find "as is," and do not make changes to force the material to agree with what you think it ought to be. Record it as you find it. Do not alter the spelling. Do not fudge the date. Retain in your notes the integrity of the document, even though you know the informational content is not "honest."

Examples of Source References

George Olin Zabriskie, *The Zabriskie Family*, Vol. I (priv. pr. 1963), p. 493.

Alfred A. Burdick, *Burdick Genealogy*, Vol. A (typescript, Baltimore, Md.), p. 196.

LeRoy F. Hafen and Ann W. Hafen, *Handcarts to Zion* (Glendale, Ca: Arthur H. Clark Co., 1960), p. 151-155.

Elizabeth Wood Thomas, "Genealogy of Lyndon Baines Johnson," *The Alabama Genealogical Register*, Vol. VI, No. 1 (Mar. 1964), p. 3-15.

Kenneth H. Thomas, Jr., "Carter-Gordy" (Georgia Family Lines), *Georgia Life*, Winter 1976, p. 40-41, 46.

Bill R. Linder, *The Linder Family in 18th Century South Carolina* (priv. pub. 1975), p. 204.

"Tribute to a Mississippi Lady," *The Murphree Quarterly*, Vol I, No. 11 (Sept. 1964), p. 90.

John H. Yates, "A History of the Yates Family," (typescript, Columbia, Mo., Univ. of Mo. Lib.), p. 47 (microfilm).

Marriage Bonds, 1829-40, Norfolk Co., Va., p. 117.

Will of Thomas Newton, 1675, York Wills, Prerogative & Exchequer Ct., Vol. 56, pt. 216.

Federal census of 1830, Warren Co., N.C., p. 39 (Nat. Arch. microfilm).

When it comes to filing, some will say they can remember well where everything is and what is in their collection, and they do not need to bother with a systematic set of record files. This can be true. Memory is our servant. We have the built-in capability of remembering anything we want to remember. Researchers who are vitally interested in their research problems and concentrate heavily on them do remember what they have searched, to whom they have written, what they have found, and where they have put the information. It is almost incredible, but true. They can do it. But these people, too, no matter how skilled they are at the use of their memory capabilities, need to set up good files and follow sound filing procedures. The reason is, someday we may all reach a stage of maturity in years where the memory is not so keen, and unfortunately or fortunately, all of us will someday die. No one has yet found a way out of this dilemma that faces genealogists! Hopefully when this happens, our records will not pass on when we do. And in order for them to be of use to others, our materials need to be properly organized and neatly filed.

The file folder and the file box or cabinet represent the most widely used filing equipment. Some use notebooks housed on shelves. From an efficiency point of view, the file folder/file cabinet method offers greater ease in handling and manipulating the material. This is the reason the business world has traditionally used this method.

The concepts of basic subject classification filing are discussed in detail in the separate chapter titled "A Total Family Records System." That chapter encourages the use of subject classification filing and the use of a "central file" in the home where all family papers are housed, and which encompasses the family genealogical files.

The first level of subject classification for filing away genealogical findings is the surname. When you begin to collect material on a family, it can be placed in a file folder labeled with the family's surname. When the file folder gets "fat," it needs to be subdivided. Files should be kept trim in order for you to use them with the greatest efficiency and effectiveness. Remember, it takes 8 times longer to file or find a piece of paper in a folder containing 50 pieces than it does in a folder containing 10 or less.

In subdividing, the most logical and genealogically useful subdivision is by locality. Records are created in localities. When we look for records, we do so by locality. Suppose after a few months of intermittent work on your Edwards family, your Edwards file folder has come to the point where the Dr. Atkins diet would do it good. Suppose that in that file the records relate mostly to Edwards relatives and ancestors from Pennsylvania. Label a new folder "EDWARDS Pennsylvania" and take all of the Pennsylvania data out of the first folder and put it in the new one. You now have two Edwards folders. The new one contains all your Edwards findings in Pennsylvania, and the other folder contains everything else you have on the Edwards family. This is the way we work with files in school, church, civic, and business offices all over the country. The same basically simple but proved efficient principles of filing are good for your genealogical files.

Let's take the subdividing of files principle a step further. When the EDWARDS Pennsylvania file becomes obese, it will need to subdivide also. Perhaps a great chunk of the Pennsylvania material is from Cumberland County. Make a new folder for just this material. Usually only one more subdivision is all that is ever needed. Your diligent research hopefully will result in a fat file of data on the Edwards in Cumberland County. You will then need to subdivide the Cumberland County material. Do it by record type this time. For example, pull out all of the census records for Cumberland County Edwards families and put them all in one folder. Or, if you have many deeds, put them all in one folder. Your labels will look like this:

EDWARDS	Pennsylvania Cumberland County Census Records

EDWARDS	Pennsylvania Cumberland County Deeds

The file folders of material you create are in essence your private home "archives" you are building on the families you are working on. Your files will contain "primary" documents relating to these family lines. However, when you analyze, evaluate, and organize information on a specific ancestor, you will isolate or pull out of the files for study those materials that relate to this particular individual. For example, your study of Benjamin Edwards may cross several of your Edwards file folders. You may want to keep together in one folder a copy or abstracts of all the information you have found relating to Benjamin Edwards—a principal ancestor you wish to especially focus your research upon. Fine. When you make a folder of information on a particular ancestor, using material from your collection of primary source documents, you should be careful to preserve the integrity of your previous research which has been carefully filed away. Do not permanently remove sheets of notes out of your primary files for inclusion in your secondary or compiled file on the one individual—unless you discipline yourself always to make cross-references to the new location for the material. The following example will help you understand the reasoning here. You may have searched all the census records for a county for a surname and placed all the notes in an appropriate folder. Later you take out of the folder the notes made on a particular man and his family, and you put it with a grouping of information on that one man. Months later you go back to your census file folder on that family in a certain locality and the files are not now complete—but you do not remember that fact! Do you see why it is important to keep your files in good order? And to make cross-references as you manipulate your files? The files will serve you better if you will use good common sense, logic, self-discipline, and good housekeeping in creating and maintaining them.

Assignment

1. Buy a box of 100 "center cut" (all tabs are in the same center position—this has been found to be more efficient than

"staggered" tabs) business-size file folders; buy a box of self-adhesive folder labels; and buy a small metal file box, a cardboard file box with a sliding drawer, or (if you can afford it and have the space for it) a good suspension metal file cabinet.

2. Go through all your genealogical notes and papers accumulated thus far and set up an efficient, organized, neat filing system—one that has no "fat" folders!

3. Reread or scan the earlier chapter on a total family records system before you start the above.

21
Evaluation Of Information

At some point you will have to evaluate the genealogical information you have found. If you are lucky, all your sources will provide the same data, but that just doesn't happen. Inconsistencies, discrepancies, and impossibilities in your sources will raise red flags signaling problems for you.

No record is perfect. You will learn to bless the memory of some clerks and curse the memory of others—the ones whose spelling was imaginative, handwriting vile, and record contents absolute guesswork. You will learn that there are good family histories and abominable ones. The eccentricities of the federal census have already been brought home to you.

In the Middle Ages monks often forged charters to establish their rights to land or exemptions from royal taxes and imposts. Their modern equivalent is the occasional unscrupulous professional or family genealogist. Be grateful that deliberate falsifications are few, however. Your problem is more likely to arise out of the incompetence or negligence of the record keeper than his fraud. Ask any lawyer you know whether the judges he deals with are more likely to be corrupt or incompetent, and he will tell you that the former are rare, while the latter are his greatest plague. It's the same with genealogists, court clerks, ministers, census takers, or the writers of diaries.

Any number of rules might be laid down. Following are a few that should be useful to you, put in the form of questions to ask yourself whenever you have to evaluate an item of genealogical data from any source.

What kind of record is it?   To answer this question you must not only be familiar with the various kinds of records useful for genealogical research (and there are many) but also be prepared to abstract from each kind every scrap of genealogically relevant material.

Original or copy?   The importance of this question is obvious. Every time a record is copied the possibility of error is increased, and you must be ready to examine the capability of the copier or copying method. Even electrostatic copy or microfilm can induce an erroneous reading; if you don't think so, see what happens when specks of dust on the copier's glass are picked up as dots, or the back of a heavily overwritten page blurs through its face on a microfilm copy.

Direct or circumstantial evidence?   Here you are looking at the record from the point of view of its usefulness in solving one or more problems. A census record may be direct evidence as to the existence of a certain family, their names, their relationships, or their ages at the time the census was taken. It is only circumstantial evidence for dates of birth of each member of the family or the date of marriage of the parents. A will is circumstantial evidence for a date of death (of the testator) and may also give clues to the ages and relationships of other persons mentioned in it. You will often find that an acceptable record is made by using a number of separate pieces of circumstantial evidence, none conclusive in itself, but together producing a "preponderance of the evidence"—lawyer's jargon for "more likely than not," and the best result you are likely to obtain. As one of the most noted American genealogists, Milton Rubincam, has said, "You cannot prove a pedigree with absolute certainty. You must base conclusions on preponderance of the evidence."

Who made the record?   Is it an official record by a court or church officer? A record in a family bible by a father? A sworn statement in a lawsuit? Was the person who made this record the person in the best position to know the facts about what he put down? Did he have a legal or moral obligation to tell the full truth? Did he have an interest in the outcome of some event which might move him to bend or conceal that full truth? Often the data in such a record must be supplied by someone else. In the case of printed family histories this is always true. Who or what was the source of each statement? Can we find out? Is it a reliable source by the other tests we have devised?

When and where was the record made?   The record nearest in time and place to the event is usually the more reliable. For example, a baptismal record made a few days after a birth (when we know that infant baptism was the practice) is always better evidence of age than a marriage record made at age 25, a census record at age 40, a deposition taken at age 60, or an entry in a son's diary after death. If a family is of German origin, a record from the village in Hesse or Bavaria will serve your purposes better than one generated in Pennsylvania or Missouri well after the event of immigration.

In the case of some classes of records there are special rules. A family bible may contain several generations of records. Look first at the publication date of the bible; if the date in question occurred before the bible was printed, you know that it was not made at the time of the event, though it may have been copied from an earlier record of the same kind. Also compare the handwriting and ink carefully; where one person has filled in a page of data covering several generations, the likelihood of error is greater.

Does the record make sense?   If the record indicates that a woman married her own brother or gave birth to a child at age 12 or 84 you can be sure that something is wrong somewhere. In the royal families of Catholic Europe, child marriages and uncle-niece marriages might often be found, whereas among the Danish peasantry even the marriage of first cousins will be unlikely. Children born too close together or too far apart are other warning signals; the former may indicate that a child has been forced into a family in which he does not belong, while the latter may direct attention to the possibility of a second wife of the same name. Col. Walter Story of Colonial Maryland had two wives named Mary and two daughters (both grew to adulthood) named Elizabeth. Under some circumstances abrupt changes in spelling may be expected (the creative imagination of English-speaking court clerks in Pennsylvania coping with the names of German immigrant families was unsurpassed) but in others they may be the sign of a badly soldered connection. Experience with the customs of the period, together with common sense, will be a great help in determining whether the son of a tanner could call himself "Gent." or vice versa, or the likely meaning of "cousin" or "Jr." or "father-in-law" in a New England will.

What other evidence do you have?   If your sources agree, and you have no conflicts, you are very likely right, and you can continue to build on the foundation of the work you have done. But be sure before you build too high that you have searched for every possible kind of relevant evidence that is available, and be ready at any time to shift your ground or tear down and rebuild when better evidence discredits what you have previously accepted. Thus your ability to evaluate evidence will require not only creative thinking in using the rules we have discussed but also in finding the data to which to apply those same rules.

22
Preparing A Short Paper

Why are you gathering up the information about the family? Usually you want to make the family story known to others. For most people, the interest does not stop at satisfying their own curiosity. They want to communicate their findings to others. They want the information to be there in the libraries and historical societies when the next generations start to look.

The communication of findings not only helps others and thereby produces a satisfying result—it has been proved many times that people are happiest when they are helping others—but it is fun to produce the written word. By all means do not regard the preparation of a short paper about one of your ancestors or on one of your family lines as "too much trouble." You have gone to a lot of trouble to find the information. Stay in the race until you cross the finish line with a final product—something for your family and friends and future generations to read.

Select as a topic material the scope of which you can easily handle in not too many pages. Some genealogical topics appropriate in a short space might be such things as a single problem of parentage, place of origin, "missing" wife or child, correction of another's work, or a summary of findings on one ancestor. Unless you are correcting, make a genuine effort to be sure the topic has not already been covered by someone else. The short paper is ideal for submitting to family magazines, to local genealogical society magazines which specialize in the area where the ancestor lived, or, if the ancestor had a far-reaching posterity, to a national genealogical publication. Such magazines do not often use extensive articles because of the demand for variety that is normally made on periodicals. You can easily make copies of short papers to distribute to family members and to deposit in the local library, historical society, and other genealogical depositories that are equipped to receive such papers. Many depositories welcome them, some actively seek them, and some are not interested. Always try to have your paper published or deposit copies in places where it can be helpful to others.

Since you are going to make your paper available to the public, you want it to be good. So, take the time to write good clean, clear English. Make sure you say what you mean. Have a literary friend look the draft over and give you suggestions for improvement. If you will be submitting the paper to a magazine for possible publication, you will need to find out in advance what requirements may exist as to style, format, citations, etc. Be courageous and try for publication. Do not be afraid your paper will be rejected because you are a newcomer. Editors are always looking for and are willing to receive good work.

Most important, always cite original sources or someone who has used them, and be sure a reader can always know the source of every fact you cite. When you draw a conclusion based on the interpretation of facts, be sure the reader knows why you have reached that conclusion. Whether right or wrong in the long run (and everyone makes mistakes), your work will be helpful to others if it follows this rule.

Before you write, be sure you have covered the ground

carefully. Find out what sources exist and consult them. If you have used the advice given in the chapter on abstracting information from documents and on notetaking and filing, you should have a good set of organized materials to work with. Preparing a short paper is made simple when the notes are well organized and neatly filed. The information almost flows right out of the files onto your paper! All you need to do is tie the notes you have made together with transition statements and an overall story line.

Start Writing Your First Paper

1. Select a first, second, or third great-grandparent about whom you will prepare a short paper. Select one for whom you have completed the research, i.e., one about whom you have exhausted the available sources for the areas in which he lived.

2. Arrange your findings in chronological order.

3. Add transition statements between the facts you have discovered, and try to make the material "tell a story." Make complete citations to the sources of the facts which you include. Make these citations at the bottom of each page or at the end.

4. The above exercise will give you good practice. Read articles in the *National Genealogical Society Quarterly* and *The American Genealogist* magazines for ideas for developing more scholarly techniques for the papers you will prepare as you continue your research.

23
Publishing A Book

A bookbinder told the author about completing a binding job of 110 books for a lady 89 years old. She had been working on the material for 35 years, but she stayed with it to the finish line. If you really want to write a book on your family or on one of your family lines, take a tip and define the scope so that you will have a stopping place. When faced with the problem of scope and ever reaching the point of being able to complete a book, the author chose to limit the scope of his work on his own surname and subsequently was able to generate a work entitled *The Linder Family of 18th Century South Carolina.* I concentrated on exhausting the South Carolina sources relating to Linders up to 1800 and then communicated my findings in a book on the subject.

Selecting the scope or the topic of the work is one of your most important considerations. It may determine whether or not the book will ever become a reality. So often ambitious researchers set out to do comprehensive genealogies, only to burn out in the process of trying to produce an overwhelming amount of research and writing. If you are compelled to do a book, give yourself a break and do a small book. If you survive the small one and are still game, then go after a telephone-directory size production.

One publisher advises that genealogists avoid "cute" titles, such as "Footprints on the Sands of Time." The title should be descriptive of the work and not catchy or dramatic. The attention-getting display title is for novels appealing to a wide audience. The published family genealogy is a professional work and a family reference work. In order for library users readily to find your material through published book lists and library catalogs, and when browsing among the shelves, the title should reflect the principal surname and locality.

Not very many published genealogies make money; getting rich is not the idea. For the most part they are a costly item. The high cost of production is pitted against the low normal distribution. It is customary to print and expect to sell 300 copies. Few sell more than that, and some have a lot left over when printing as few as 300. Published genealogies have a limited market. We go to the trouble of publishing family genealogies not for monetary profit but for the great experience it is for the compiler-author and for the benefit it offers to others. Family pride is perhaps the chief motivator—and a worthy one.

As with any writing, use good clear English in the text. As has been advised before, use source references. Completely identify your sources. Keep fact and conclusion or speculation separate. Avoid complicated numbering systems. Embellish the book with photographs, maps, documents, etc., as available and appropriate and as cost permits. You want to bring the people to life as best you can. Strive to make a genuine contribution, not just a skeleton of the family.

Your book should be published on a good quality non-acidic paper. Ask for "grade D buckram" for the best hardback binding; however, grade C is perfectly O.K. and costs less. The "perfect" binding (paper-back) is where the back is shredded, glue added, and a cover put around it. These are some of the things you will discuss with your publisher. Your objectives and the costs will enter into your final decisions as to paper and binding. Published genealogies generally have a preface and an introduction. The preface is normally written by the author. It gives the mechanics, how the book is organized, and may describe or explain the research undertaken. When an introduction is included, it is more often than not written by some other person in the field and serves to introduce the author and the work from the viewpoint of another individual. This person may be paid a fee and/or presented with one or two complimentary copies of the book. Following the text, be sure to include an index. True, indexes are a lot of work to create, but yes, they are essential.

The method of publication involves some decisions. Will it be hot lead or cold type offset printing? Offset is the most feasible today because it is cheaper and you have easier proofing. With this method you prepare "camera-ready" (that is, typed and ready to photograph) copy, usually on 8½" x 11" paper, using a carbon ribbon typewriter, with sufficient margins for photographic reduction, and using pica type. Camera-ready guide sheets are normally available from the publisher, or he can give you guidance on recommended top and side margins for preparing the typed copy. Of course, if funds are available, an attractive "vanity book," complete with set type, color, etc., can be published.

Recommended Reading

Meredith B. Colket, Jr., "Creating a Worthwhile Family Genealogy," *National Genealogical Society Quarterly*, Vol. 56, No. 4 (December 1968), available in reprint for $2 from the National Genealogical Society, 1921 Sunderland Place N.W., Washington, DC 20036.

part four
Hiring Or Becoming
A Skilled Genealogist

24
Hiring A
Researcher

There are numerous persons skilled at genealogical research who do research for a fee, and the numbers increase each year as the field develops. These individuals for the most part work independently, and there exists a great variety in skill levels. In order to help the public know who is capable of what and as an aid to the genealogical researchers, a group of interested genealogists formed the Board for Certification of Genealogists in 1964. This Board formulates standards of genealogical research, receives applications for several categories of researchers, and determines whether the applicant will be "certified" to perform certain functions. Those who are certified are placed on lists or registers of competent genealogists, lineage specialists, and genealogical records searchers.

A "genealogist" as termed by the Board is one who not only conducts research among primary sources and studies secondary sources, but also constructs genealogies of families based upon his investigation of the sources and careful analysis of the evidence.

An "American lineage specialist" is a genealogist who prepares a lineage (single line of descent) and is competent to determine the authenticity of evidence and acceptability of original source material and compiled and printed material. A "genealogical record searcher" is one who searches original records (census records, wills, deeds, military records, pensions, etc.) but who makes no attempt to reconstruct a pedigree or to prepare a family history. Successful applicants are authorized to place the initials "C.G." (Certified Genealogist), "C.A.L.S." (Certified American Lineage Specialist), or "G.R.S." (Certified Genealogical Record Searcher) after their names.

The Genealogical Society of Utah also has what it calls a system of "accrediting" genealogists, thus you may find a genealogist with the initials "A.G." following his name. Persons who wish to become accredited by the Genealogical Society and appear on its accreditation listings prove their merit by evidencing their work and taking an examination. Researchers are accredited for research in specific localities, such as England, Sweden, or New England states. The Board for Certification mentioned earlier deals only with research in the United States and Canada.

Most genealogists and records searchers, including those who have been certified by the Board, those who have been accredited by the Genealogical Society, and those who work without having been either certified or accredited, advertise their services in genealogical publications. *The Genealogical Helper* magazine, the most widely circulated genealogical publication, contains in each issue numerous display and classified advertisements placed by persons who do genealogical research for a fee. Some of the best or more noted genealogists do not need to advertise. They have an established clientele, and their skills and services are made known by word of mouth.

Many foreign researchers advertise their services in American publications, but since there is no international organization setting forth standards or governing the field, one must be cautious when hiring research done in foreign countries. It is good to first try small assignments for small investments. If you are satisfied with the report and the fee, fine, then proceed.

Be advised that hiring someone to do research for you is an expensive matter. It is always better to do the work yourself if at all possible. But when you must hire a researcher, it is wise to set a fee basis at the outset. Be sure you understand the terms. Record searchers are paid by the hour; genealogists may charge by the hour at a higher rate or they may set a project fee. You will usually be asked to pay for travel and other expenses, but you should have the right to approve these in advance if they are substantial sums.

Unless specifically agreed, you are not paying on a reward basis (no result, no fee) and you may spend large sums for work with small results. The better the work and reputation of the genealogist, the more you may expect to pay. You should receive written reports, and the information obtained for you is your property. If the researcher wishes to publish it, he must seek your permission first.

The initial letter of inquiry to a genealogist or record searcher is important. Keep it clear and simple. Do not overwhelm him on first contact with a large envelope or box of material relating to your problem. Let the relationship develop in a business-like way. He will ask you questions and instruct you as to what he needs.

Recommended Learning Experience

1. Write for information about the Board for Certification of Genealogists and a list of certified individuals: 1307 New Hampshire Ave. N.W., Washington, DC 20036.

2. Scan an issue of *The Genealogical Helper*, noting the advertisements placed by genealogists advertising their services.

25
Educational Opportunities

Since 1950 the National Archives has sponsored an intensive three-week genealogical education program, called the National Institute on Genealogical Research. This program was undertaken by the National Archives to help develop the skills of persons engaged in tracing family trees. The goal was prompted by the fact that this body of researchers had consistently been the largest block of users of the National Archives.

The National Institute on Genealogical Research consists of lectures, workshop sessions, field trips, and a research project. Lecturers are leading genealogists, historians, and archivists. There are both guest lecturers and National Archives staff lecturers. The course is designed for persons who have had some experience and are beyond the beginner stage.

Many of the leading contributors in the field of genealogy today are former students of the National Institute on Genealogical Research. The three-week course is normally held once annually during the last three weeks of July. It is held in the National Archives building in Washington, DC. Students are responsible for their own housing. The number of students is limited to 50, and enrollments are accepted on a first-come first served basis. Information can be obtained from the Office of Educational Programs, National Archives, Washington, DC 20408.

There are regionally based educational programs. The New England Historic Genealogical Society sponsors an educational program in connection with Harvard University. Samford University, Birmingham, Ala., sponsors a one-week program each June in which classes are offered for beginning, intermediate, and advanced skill levels. Brigham Young University, Provo, Utah, sponsors a one-week program each August which draws the largest crowds (3,000 in 1976) and provides the widest selection of class offerings. In the summer of 1978 a new one-week annual institute was successfully launched in Texas—the Houston Genealogical Institute, P.O. Box 12938, Houston, TX 77017.

There are numerous special workshops and seminars sponsored on an ad hoc basis by various groups throughout the country each year. Such seminars are frequently held in connection with the annual meetings of genealogical societies. Some societies sponsor special lectures during their program seasons. These seminars and special programs are generally advertised in genealogical periodicals, genealogical columns in newspapers, and through special mailings to members of the sponsoring societies.

The adult education programs of colleges or of local government educational organizations often offer genealogy classes for beginners. Many church groups and other organizations sponsor genealogy classes. An organization of genealogical educators was formed recently. For information, write to the Librarian, Prof. F. Wilbur Helmbold, Samford University, Birmingham, AL 35209.

Genealogical Study Tours Abroad

The author periodically sponsors genealogical study tours in Britain for U.S. genealogists. The program normally consists of several days of classes taught by leading British genealogists, field trips to research depositories, sightseeing trips, and time for research. When a study-research tour will be held in a given year, it is advertised in genealogical magazines and columns. Inquiries can be addressed to: Genealogy Tour to Britain, c/o R. H. Linder, 109 West Main Street, Kenedy, Texas 78119, and they will be forwarded.

The Brigham Young University Department of Travel Study, Provo, Utah, often sponsors a genealogical study tour to Britain with a departure from Salt Lake City. Research guidance and consultation are provided at the outset, but classes are not offered.

Is it Possible to Plan a Career in Genealogy?

Realistically speaking, the opportunities for a career in genealogy are few; and the income prospects from doing research for a fee are normally inadequate for the comfortable support of a family.

The national, state, and local archives, libraries, and historical societies have staff members who assist the genealogical public and answer their mail requests, but seldom are these attendants and reference employees termed "genealogists." They are, however, often given training to help them understand and meet the needs of genealogical researchers; but, for the most part, these people are really archivists, historians, and librarians. Their jobs are generally financially supported by the public. In some cases, such as many historical societies, the jobs are supported by private charitable contributions. In either case, funds for salaries are limited and are usually substandard when compared with private industry.

The Genealogical Society in Salt Lake City employs several hundred persons; however, these positions are quite specialized. Most of the employees do not "do genealogy" per se. Here and there around the country there are universities that sponsor genealogical education programs, for which directors are required. Such programs are often part of larger programs, however, and do not have independent status, and the directors are often administrative types.

In and around Salt Lake City there has developed a small industry of research firms, and firms specializing in publishing indices have also come into existence. These are all small firms, usually employing no more than a few persons.

In some cases people interested in genealogy have been able to build an income from publishing genealogical books or periodicals; but conversations with these people indicate that a real love of the work has to be involved to keep things going.

Those who do research for a fee normally are supplementing their incomes, doing it as part-time work, or doing it for something to do that they enjoy. Retired persons, housewives, and single persons without families to support make up the bulk of persons who do research for a fee.

It is difficult to make a living at research because of the limit the traffic will stand in hourly rates. Even if the researcher is successfully able to charge a high hourly rate, there is the problem of maintaining a steady slate of business day after day and week after week.

This author advises anyone who is genuinely interested in pursuing a career associated with genealogy, to study history, library science, business management, or all three. Then go to work in one of these fields. Work on your genealogy as an avocation and become skilled and masterful in it. In the process of your research, attending seminars, reading the current materials, and meeting people in the field, watch for any opportunities that may come up where you can combine your career talents and genealogical skills in some soul-satisfying full-time job.

Even better advice would be temporarily to forget about a career in genealogy. Instead, enthusiastically and energetically throw yourself into one of the most lucrative fields you can find, adapt to, and enjoy. Make your million, then spend your time overseeing your investments, doing your genealogical research and writing, and monitoring the various needed indexing and publishing projects you have selected to endow as your special contribution to the field of genealogy.

Suggestions

1. Find out from someone you know, from a librarian, or from *The Genealogical Helper* or other periodical, if there is a class, seminar, or other program you can attend near your home.

2. Write for a brochure describing the National Institute on Genealogical Research sponsored by the National Archives. Even if you are unable to attend the Institute, study the course offerings and become familiar with the names of the lecturers.

3. Meet and talk with at least two professional genealogists about their work. Make your visit an in-depth interview if possible. Also interview people who work in depositories which serve the genealogical public. Find out how these people feel about their jobs. Ask those with whom you visit for counsel about a genealogy-connected career.

Epilogue

The pursuit of genealogy, now enjoyed by thousands (perhaps millions if we had a good count), is today one of the world's most popular indoor hobbies. The ranks of searchers are filled with interesting, friendly people who are researching for fun and relaxation. Those who get into it have a great time, and, once under way, they generally continue the pursuit throughout their lifetimes.

As you do research, you will use the experience and prior research of others to get your start. You will consult many of the thousands of published genealogies and indices created by others long before you became interested. You will be drawing from the world of genealogy. Plan also to be a contributor. Participate in your local genealogical group. Accept an assignment. Volunteer to help index or preserve records needing attention. Publish your own findings. When you become experienced yourself, motivate, encourage, and assist others. Start a group, or teach a beginner's class.

As you join in and participate, be a positive, creative addition. Be happy, friendly, and cooperative. Help make working in the field of genealogy one of the most enjoyable experiences a person can have. Now go to work. You will enrich your life and have a grand time.

BILL R. LINDER